Published in the United States by
Screaming Armadillo Comedy LLC

Life Improvised: Listening Between the Lines

www.ScreamingArmadilloComedy.com

eBook ISBN: 978-1-7362383-0-1
Paperback ISBN: 978-1-7362383-1-8

THE CREATIVES

Amanda Donahue/The Scribblist (Cover and Section Art)
www.thescribblist.com

Cynthia Goodman (editor) Radiantcyn@aol.com

Any remaining errors add to the street vibe of this publication.

I0138693

LIFE IMPROVISED
Listening Between the Lines

GREG PHILIPPI

DEDICATIONS

SPECIAL THANK YOU
I would like to dedicate this book to my wife Sara. Sara Philippi has been my partner for many years and my rock. Sara, you have been my guiding light and strength on even the darkest nights. We've laughed and cried together and been through much on this journey. You have my heart.

I'd like to thank Arlee Thornhill, my mentor and guide. Your wisdom, love and friendship I will carry with me while I am on this plane. I'm so proud to be, as you said, your other son. Thank you Rob Fava, for your big heart, hidden ever so slightly under that New York edge, your wacky humor, and daily creative nudging, Cynthia Goodman for providing feedback and a light at the end of the tunnel, Amanda Donahue (front cover and section art; www.thescribblist.com) for believing in me and going above and beyond creatively for me. Your insight is appreciated and your art is amazing!

Thanks to my early improv mentors and coaches; David Razowsky, you were my introduction to this art form through Second City and a beacon in the fog. Thanks to Bill Chott (the ImprovTrick, iO West), for your friendship, clear concise direction and always positive attitude, Tom Booker (Second City, Annoyance Theater) you believed in me and showed me my writing potential all those years ago, Monkey Butler Comedy Improv Los Angeles, for giving my heart and soul a home away from home and providing a support group during tough times, Stacey Smith (iO Theater & Boston Improv) for your musical improv inspiration and to the Upright Citizens Brigade for taking me to new horizons.

Last but not least, special thanks to all those who've taken a Screaming Armadillo Comedy class or workshop or come to me for private coaching. Fellow Armadillos, you are awesome!

WHY IMPROV
AN INTRODUCTION

Why improv? Ask yourself, why air? Why does chicken soup taste so good when you're sick? Why are eggplants smooth and purple? Why?! I'll tell you why "because" that's why. Improv is as natural as breathing and you get the benefits of several cloves of garlic without the negatives, like bad breath and gastric issues. Perhaps the first question should be what is improv?

Improvisation, or improv, is a form of live theatre in which the plot, characters and dialogue of a game, scene or story are made up in the moment. Often improvisers will take a suggestion from the audience or draw on some other source of inspiration to get started.

Many students sign up for improv classes because they think improv is about being funny. It's not. Improv is about being interesting. Finding the funny can be part of your improv quest, just know, there are powerful improv scenes that are not funny at all. Great improv is engaging and holds your interest-- whether funny or not, and it tells a story. Often the simplest moments are the most powerful ones.

WHO IS GREG PHILIPPI?
Who is author Greg Philippi? I was just asking myself that very question and will continue to do so for the remainder of this life. Every time I think I know myself I discover something new about Greg. Improv is a big part of that discovery process.

Author Greg Philippi once swam with a giant green sea turtle off the Maui coast. Greg also once appeared on the television show "Charmed," as head of the Demon Village. His mother just shook her head and brought him another bowl of pea soup…ah, but we're getting ahead of ourselves and it was a tiny role anyhow. First things first. Let's start at the beginning. Everything starts at the beginning-- except a great improv scene.

Improv scenes NEVER should start at the beginning. Improv scenes always should start in the middle of the action. "I've been waiting half an hour for you. You've been late three times this week. No matter-- I ordered you a drink." With this information we know where the scene partners are. We also know that one is extremely late and that their lateness is a common occurrence. We also know the two meet often and that the improviser who arrived early has a forgiving heart cause he or she ordered the other a drink. All that can be garnered from a couple lines plus the action is already in play.

Having trained at several improv schools I've been exposed to a myriad of approaches to the craft. While each methodology differs slightly in execution and some in terminology, the goal to create great scenes is a constant.

The more I've studied improv, the more evident it's become to me, that my life parallels an improv scene. Understanding that scene can not only make me a better improviser but a better person as well.

THE PURPOSE OF THIS BOOK

As I take you through elements of improv in this book, peppered with stories from my life, you may see parallels with your own life. The intended take-away is that we humans are all connected, even more so if you're an improviser because improvisers embrace the concept of group mind. It's that connection a team has onstage when all pistons are firing. If all of us are connected, shouldn't we all support one another? Shouldn't we all have each other's back? The answer is, yes. Very much so. When you make your scene partner look good you look good.

Improvisers are also actors. Well-rounded improvisers are much more. They're historians and philosophers, poets and painters. They dabble in knowledge and all things creative and are constantly growing and expanding their mind.

When you break down the word improviser, the sum of its individual parts are the pieces that make the whole. **IM** is **I am** and translates as the improviser who is confident and grounded. **PRO** becomes **good at being myself** to the point of exuding professional excellence, especially when I am on stage, and **VISER** translates to being **blessed with vision and focused on the aspect of discovery**. If you ever wonder what you're doing in improv, perhaps reading over the above words will help!

IM = I am **PRO** = being good at being myself **VISER** = with focused vision!

Improv is about communication and agreement and listening and opening one's self up to the many possibilities of the universe that will allow creativity to flow to and from us. Improv is about getting to know ourselves just a little better each day.

All things communicate. You might ask yourself; how can a rock communicate? Innate objects have a vibration. Vibrations are communication. All things communicate. Of course, in an improv scene, two rocks can also have a conversation. Imagine how fascinating that might be? "You know Clarence I've been standing here all day. Is it too much to ask for a little shade?"

So often in improv we think and play in linear terms. But improv is not bound by the rules of a linear three-dimensional world. Why limit your state of play? Life is an improv scene and our best moments are delivered unscripted and from the heart. Life on stage and off reflects upon itself.

PUTTING KNOWLEDGE TO WORK

What if you find yourself in a scene about something that you have no knowledge of? For me that would be certain sports, okay, most sports. In that instance, play to the truth of what you do know and what you think may be true. The gravelly walk to the football stadium, and your date in heels, or the fact that you're seated so far away that the team are just specs and you thought it only happened at rock concerts. Try to play to what you do know about.

If as an improviser you make a statement that is non-factual, yet you have committed to the scene and spoken from your heart thinking it was true, you will still get points for not going for the joke. You'll probably get a laugh. If you are committed to doing your best and playing the scene truthfully, your scene will be interesting for all its inconsistencies regarding the subject matter, because what you said was delivered innocently, in truth.

I was directing a show featuring some mid-level improvisers. One woman stepped out and her character made a comment about a baseball players' batting average, but she named a famous American football player. She evidently had no idea the football player was not a baseball player, and the crowd ate it up. They were rolling in the aisles with laughter.

Improv is the study of humans and human interaction on stage and in real time. A great improviser is someone who can view the world from many different angles and show others the skewed viewpoint they have just witnessed. Great improvisers are also constantly learning more about not only the world, but about themselves. It takes courage to dig deep and learn more about yourself. If you do, you will become a better improviser.

Through improv you can play with the most absurd concepts including multiple dimensions like one where talking eggplants dance at a barbecue, as farm animals are grilling other veggies. Of course, it's all played seriously, in a world that accepts the unusual. Just please don't name me as one of the veggies being grilled.

A fascinating aspect of improv is that you can step on an improv stage and play like a child, yet deal with time travel, death, rebirth, multi dimensions and other adult themes.

There's also the aspect of improv in your everyday life. Learning to identify the elements of improv as you go about your daily routine can be both challenging and rewarding. Perhaps this book will shed some light on how to process those elements and use them to your advantage.

BOUNDARIES

Improv has no boundaries except those you put on your creative thought. In improv you can fly, you can talk with animals or be one. In improv your spirit can live inside an innate object, travel through time, raise the dead, and see thought as a living breathing thing. Therefore, it's safe to say that through improv, everything is possible.

Some say there are no rules in improv. To make such a statement wouldn't be a truthful one. There are numerous unwritten rules in improv. If you don't follow them your scenes will die an ugly death. Perhaps a painful one. Of course, experienced improvisers that have mastered these unwritten rules may need to break those same rules occasionally, while reaching forward to blaze new trails-- and that's okay as well.

While mastering the unwritten rules of the improv world everyone should dare to fail! Reach for the stars, take chances. We are all in this lifeboat together. For many of you, this may be a review, but to those just getting started, here are a few of the unwritten rules of improv: **"YES"**, **"YES AND"**, **"DO NOT DENY"** and remember-- **"the scene is about your relationship with your scene partner"**. Nothing more, nothing less. Ok we're done. You can close this book and go home.

"YES" In the beginning, there was yes. Yes, is the acceptance of whatever concept or statement that improviser numero uno makes to improviser dos. **"YES AND!"** Once the two improvisers in the scene are in agreement, the second improviser replies with an added bit of information to help move the scene forward. **"YES AND"** is Tina Fey's mantra. For those uninitiated, Tina Fey is ex-SNL and a writer, producer, actor and all-around improv bad ass. So **"YES AND"** is acceptance with an added something to propel the scene forward.

"DO NOT DENY" If I tell you I am wearing purple shoes, do not tell me I should get glasses because I am wearing blue shoes, or that I am not wearing shoes at all. You accept the concept that's been established. If I say I'm enjoying staring at the full moon, you cannot say that there is no full moon, that I must be mistaken. You're in a scene and your scene partner seems to be staring; "Mark, that's a lovely purple dress you're wearing." You may be unhappy your scene partner just put you in a dress but as an improviser you must accept that you are wearing a purple dress. "I always wanted the freedom that pants don't allow and I saw it on sale at Nordstrom" is an acceptable response. "You need glasses Glen, I'm in shorts" is not acceptable.

HOW TO USE THIS BOOK
In this book, I will share my take on Improv theory and techniques, and my life experiences, while encouraging you to reach deep within yourself and to experiment with new creative concepts both onstage and off. You can read *Life Improvised* from cover to cover or just home in on chapters that speak to you. Either way you'll benefit.

FORMS OF IMPROV- LONG AND SHORT
Some of you may be wondering what is long form improv and what is short form improv? Think either "Whose Line Is It Anyway?" style improv games and short scenes for short form improv, or a one act play that is totally made up on the spot, for long form improv. Know that Long and Short form improv use different parts of the brain. In using this book you'll be working both the analytical and creative sides of the brain.

There are also varying styles of long form play. Short form is usually either game play competition or scene based with games. You'll have the opportunity to explore new long form styles as you move forward. The most important point to note is that through this book and through the classes you take, your instructor should be a conduit for your energy sparking your creativity and intensifying your creative flow.

Improv is about telling stories, and it's about truth, your truth. No two actors play a villain or hero the same way. Each brings something unique to the role. It's the same with improv. Remember *YOU ARE THE ONLY YOU* and that is the one thing any improviser brings to the improv stage that nobody else can. You bring yourself!

IN MEMORY OF ROBIN

I had this student who attended my drop-in class every week for at least a year, without improvement. She just wasn't particularly good at improv. Her go-to always reverted to sex in some uncomfortable way and was not funny. Our chats before and after class revealed her to be a talented, creative, thoughtful person with much more depth than showed in her improv play. I wrestled with how I might help her be a stronger improviser. She seemed to have the smarts, but she just wasn't connecting.

However, she kept coming to class, and finally her skills began to improve. Suddenly she was committing to the scene and had become passionate and engaging in her work on stage. I complimented her on her improvement. It was as if someone had waved a magic wand or turned on a light switch and Robin was blossoming into a talented improviser. Robin was connecting with her scene partner and having strong meaningful scenes.

One evening before class, Robin came in early, and presented me with the most beautiful hand-made cufflinks. Robin said she'd been contracted to sell her custom cufflinks at a high-end department store and wanted me to have a pair. I was thrilled. The cufflinks were exceptionally detailed and the design with its tiny gears showcased her creative flair. After handing me the cufflinks, she pulled me aside and told me that I had changed her life. I asked her what she meant. She repeated that I had changed her life and added that I was a miracle worker. "How so?" I inquired. She explained that I taught her about herself, enabling her to know who she is.

I paused for a moment, then said, *I didn't change your life. You did. You changed your own life. I was merely the conduit for that change.* I repeated that statement and then explained to Robin that she took the time to listen and to learn about herself. I merely provided a framework for her to express herself within. She smiled. I went on holiday, looking forward to seeing even more growth from Robin when I returned, since her scene work had come so far.

However, when I returned several weeks later, I learned that the weekend before I'd returned, Robin had gone on an improv cruise. The day after getting back, Robin had a sudden massive heart attack and died. It was a shock to me and to the improv community in general. Robin's radiance and creativity are missed, but her memory is forever preserved in the smiles and laughter of all my students.

As you read through this book, I'm hoping you find ways to use it to improve your work both on and off stage. I'm also hoping you'll use this book to learn more about yourself and who you are as an improviser and as a person, and like Robin, use my words for growth. Many blessings to you Robin. See you on the other side.

Table of Contents

PART THREE
DARE TO FAIL!

PART ONE

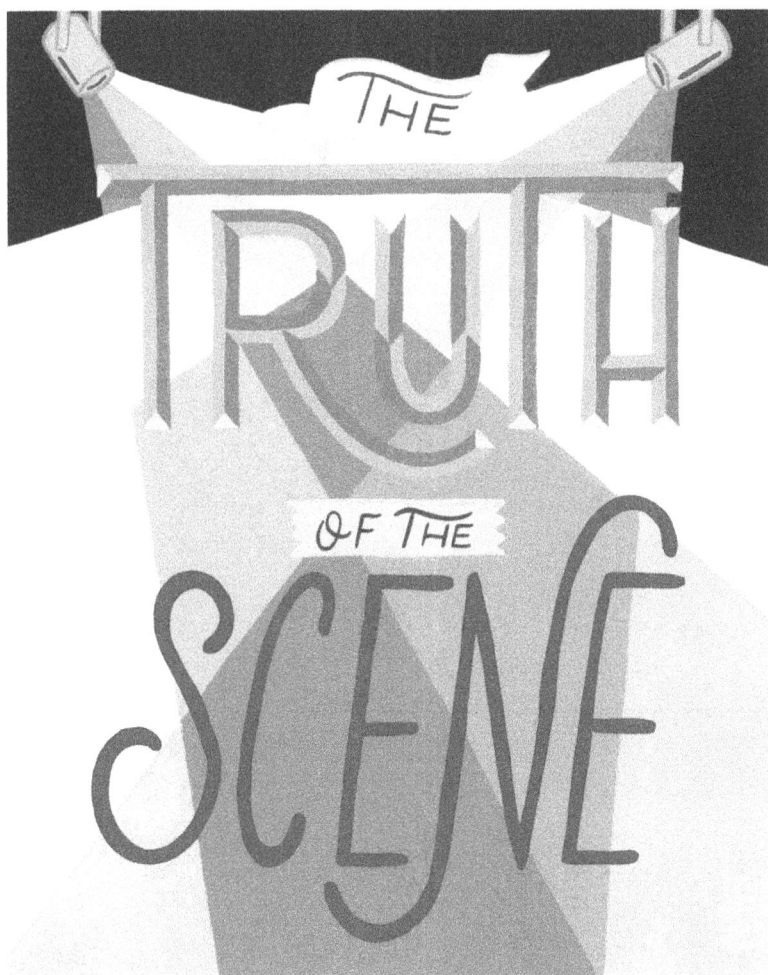

THE TRUTH OF THE SCENE

WORDS MATTER

"I have been many things in life: A trader walking barefoot through the jungle. A medical doctor driving to his clinic in a shiny Mercedes and to the surprise of many and above all myself, a Hollywood actor. But nothing has shaped my life as much as surviving the Pol Pot Regime. I am a survivor of the Cambodian holocaust. That's who I am." -Haing Ngor (Academy Award Winner Best Supporting Actor for "The Killing Fields, A Cambodian Odyssey")

In improv scenes we often don't give any thought to the words that come out of our mouths. Often our characters just keep talking, continuing beyond making simple statements, in an attempt to fill every last crevice with bloviation. Not only do we talk too much, but we don't take the time to think about the words we're using. Ah, the words…the power of words.

I'd seen *The Killing Fields* and was moved by the performance of Haing Ngor. At the time, I was working in television, had read a bit about his extraordinary background, and found his performance to be natural and emotionally stirring, that I felt compelled to reach out to him. So, I tracked down Haing Ngor's address, and wrote him a personal letter. My letter found Haing living in a modest apartment in Chinatown, on the outskirts of downtown Los Angeles. He wrote me back personally. I was touched and thrilled to get his letter. Though letter was short, his words were powerful, and more importantly-- so was the energy that came with them. I read it over several times and still, I cherish his reply, written without ego and from the heart.

Words carry weight, yet we throw them around without giving any thought to the power they wield. Your improv scene partner has just made a short statement. You take a moment and digest what your scene partner has said and respond thoughtfully. You hope your scene partner feels your words and the emotion that travels with them, so they can respond in kind, just as you hope they would respond in your everyday life. In an improv scene as in life, words are powerful. Words do not only carry weight, but the same words spoken several different ways can carry much different messages.

THE CAR DEALERSHIP

I was buying a car, and as I sat doing paperwork in the finance office, I noticed a large tire by the finance guy's desk. It had a large chunk missing from the side of the tire. The whole thing was a display to advertise great extended warranty coverage.

The finance guy saw me looking at the tire and said, "I'm trying to have someone remove that display from my office. I mean who does that to a tire anyway?" I answered, "Well I have." Three simple words. Everyone who was there in the office with me probably realized that the curb does bite occasionally, and somebody might have an extremely bad day behind the wheel like I once did. They all laughed.

The car finance guy went on about that tire display in his office, without realizing what he was saying. He was paying no attention to the words coming from his mouth. My three words spoke to the situation, everyone got it, and it was funny. Just three words were important enough. It's amazing how just a couple words can carry such power. Six months later I hit a curb and took a chunk out of my new cars front tire that was quite large. Buy the extended warranty coverage.

WORDS IN IMPROV STYLES

There are fast pace and slow pace improv styles. Before playing a fast-paced improv scene, tune your mind to accept a faster vibration and anticipate a faster scene rhythm. The words still carry the same emotional intensity and meanings, even though there isn't much time to digest the words spoken in the scene. That's okay. Remember, words carry weight and you are reacting truthfully. You may only have time to replay some of your scene partner's words in your mind before responding. You may only have time to replay a feeling you got when he or she spoke. Try to think about what intention the words carried and respond to that emotional intent. If your mind is blank, then agree

2

with your scene partner, and do your best to add some additional bit of information. Just simply practice "yes and".

In slow paced improv, when there is more time to digest the words and respond with emotional intent, you still might find yourself at a loss when responding. As an improviser, remember to think about how you feel, and keep your response short.

Realize the weight of your words in all situations. How much credence do you give to the words that come from your mouth? How often do you really listen to what your scene partner is saying, or to what your friends are saying, or to your life partner outside of class? There are times you can convey words without even speaking them.

Words spoken from the heart, on and off stage, have power. Words in an improv scene with no emotion, ring hollow. Those same words spoken in a scene with emotion, have immense power. They could carry an excited, happy, sad or angry vibration that would connect the characters on stage.

Haing Ngor knew the power of words. He'd seen countries, leaders, regimes taken down by words. He'd felt the loss of loved ones, and their last words shared, lingered in his brain. Haing Ngor had seen the loss of freedom when no one used any words to speak out.

The Killing Fields was a British biographical drama. It was a film about the Khmer Rouge regime in Cambodia, which is based on the experiences of two journalists. The film begins during the Vietnam War and continues through the occupation and cleansing of Cambodia by a brutal murderous regime. Haing Ngor earned an Oscar for his work on *The Killing Fields* in which he relived the Cambodian holocaust on screen.

The Killing Fields won 5 BAFTA awards (British Academy of Film and Television Awards), one Golden Globe, one Writers Guild Award, 2

National Society of Film Critics Awards and 3 Academy Awards including Haing Ngor's win for best supporting actor, as well as a Golden Globe for Best Supporting Actor-Motion Picture.

Before the war, Haing Ngor had been a successful surgeon. Since arriving in the U.S. and even with his work onscreen Haing Ngor continued to live humbly, acting as a living example of the principals his words carried, which he believed in for all.

Several months after I received my letter from Haing Ngor, he was gunned down while working in his garden. It was an execution style killing. The local and overseas Cambodian community nearly unanimously believe that Ngor's outspoken advocacy for simple freedoms across Asia, his words, were why he was fatally shot outside his apartment. Ngor was only 55 years old.

Investigators, however, did not uncover evidence of a political hit, and three local gang members eventually were convicted of murder. Perhaps the why of Haing Ngor's murder will never be totally exposed. Maybe it's no longer important. At the time, the American Thai community was speaking out against corruption in Thailand and throughout Asia. The pen is mightier than the sword. Let your words be your bond.

Choose your words carefully but let them flow from your heart not your head. Be affected by an emotional connection to your scene partner and what they have just said. If your words not only make an emotional connection but they come from your skewed viewpoint, the humor will lodge itself deeply in its mark.

Today, the niece that Haing Ngor carried out of Cambodia while escaping their Khmer Rouge captors, has possession of his Oscar. In his autobiography, Haing Ngor describes his journey with his niece as a harrowing one-- dodging land mines and eating rats for food. "This is for you. I did this for you," he told her after his win at the Academy Awards. Speak to the scene and from your heart when you can.

BELIEVABLE CHOICES

Improv is all about choices. Our everyday lives are also made up of choices. Making believable choices in improv doesn't mean you have to make boring choices. Yet so often, we do mainly because boring choices are safe choices. Why? As grownups we're taught that safe choices are good. In improv safe choices are a curse. In life when not making safe choices we also often make insincere choices. We go half in. It's another safe path. So why do we make insincere choices? Is it fear? Perhaps. Bad habits? Could be.

On stage, strong committed choices equal strong scenes. Perhaps you should look at the choices you make in your everyday life first. Ask yourself, "am I making an effort to make strong choices in my life?" We are all human, so choices we make may not always be the right choices. However, believable, sincere choices are strong choices and making strong choices means you are taking control of your life offstage or the scene onstage. Don't let the fear of making a wrong choice or the rigid boundaries your parents or your job put on you dictate the choices you make or whether you even make a choice at all. Choose.

I was finishing a meal at City Wok, a Studio City California casual Chinese eatery (basically Chinese with a healthy twist). The restaurant was bustling and full of both studio employees and non-entertainment diners. Frank Gorshin, an iconic character actor, was seated two tables over, dining with a friend. He finished his meal and left just before me. You might be familiar with Gorshin and his portrayal of "The Riddler" in the 60's *Batman* series. In life, he was much more. As I headed for my car on that cool dry evening, I passed him standing alone on the curb, staring at the sky, and smoking. It was a rare clear L.A. night and the stars were overhead. We were alone in the parking lot.

Frank Gorshin straddled the worlds of improv, acting and stand-up comedy. He was a character actor, comedian and impressionist with many guest appearances on the *Ed Sullivan* and *Steve Allen Shows*.

Gorshin's "Riddler" in the original *Batman* series of the mid 1960s, has been defined as the consummate Riddler character portrayal. More importantly, Frank Gorshin was perfecting improvised dialogue before improv had ever reached the mainstream. He had perfected building realistic characters as well, giving them life, often surprising and delighting audiences.

Frank Gorshin was also the epitome of applying improv to life onstage and off. When he did a scene, he boldly wrapped himself around the character and inserted himself into the scene 150%. His characters were intense.

I wanted to say something, to have a conversation, while standing next to him outside the restaurant, but I respected his space. The man was timeless looking. He hadn't aged. I started to speak but caught myself. No, not tonight. It felt that it was such a personal moment for Frank Gorshin as he stared into the night. I decided I'd just give Frank a compliment rather than attempt to start a long conversation. I stopped next to him for a moment and praised his work, remembering the layered characters he'd portrayed on numerous TV and film guest starring roles, including his brilliant "Riddler" character. There's something about a colleague praising your work with a few words about the characters you've created, rather than just "oooohing" and "aaaaahing" like an over the top fan, that makes a colleague's praise acceptable, giving credibility to the compliment.

Gorshin turned to me, slowly cracked a smile, and without ego, thanked me. It was as if the world stopped and we were in suspended animation. You could see on Frank's face that his life to this point hadn't been about the money or the fame, but the satisfaction of a job well done. It was a clear quiet evening. Frank Gorshin then turned around, back to his stargazing, and once again focused inward.

A successful improv show or a successful scene in class is all about making connections and exploring what the improviser is feeling inside. A successful improv scene involves scene partners connecting with one another and with their environment. A successful scene is a slice of life and the shiny objects we encounter living it. I could see that behind Gorshin's eyes, the wheels were turning in his brain. We were having a scene on that evening. A short scene.

A week later, Frank Gorshin was dead of lung cancer. I didn't even know that he'd been sick. He didn't seem sick, but his countenance revealed that he knew he'd drawn the short stick and his time was up. That night on the curb, Frank Gorshin was taking stock of his journey. He'd given 150%!

Gorshin's characters were BIG but real, believable and easy to digest. His commitment to the truth of each and every project, was immense and unwavering! Are you ready to do work on this scale? It starts by making choices, believable choices, and then committing to those choices.

In improv, GO BIG! Take chances in your improv scenes. Support your scene partner! Dare to fail! There is a difference however, between going "big" and playing unreal characters that cannot be justified in the scene. There is no place in improv for characters that might bring the improviser a quick laugh but kill the scene or make their scene partner look bad. When I write "go big," I'm urging you to go all in--to really commit.

Believe in your choices, and others will. Remember, if you introduce something unusual to the fabric of the scene, if you treat it as truth, and your scene partner reacts seriously as though it were a truth, then it becomes that truth. What you've introduced into the scene, your choices, are now part of the reality on stage-- as long as you continue to justify your choices.

MAKING BELIEVABLE CHOICES
Let's look at a couple examples of believable choices. Your scene suggestion is "Sunrise". The scene opens with one of the scene partners swirling an umbrella in their drink. "Glad you could make it. I've ordered you a Tequila Sunrise. I can pick your brain easier after a few drinks." Normal and believable. Now let's take believable a bit

further; "Glad you could make it. Of course, it's not like you had a choice. We go over the hill at Sunrise and many of us won't be coming back." Greater stakes but still believable.

Here's another believable choice that has stakes regarding the suggestion "sunrise"; "Rope too tight? You won't feel anything at Sunrise when your horse rides off and leaves you danglin'." It's a dark choice but still a believable choice.

Taking the suggestion of sunrise, a bit further; "Being part of our colony means standing up to a bit of a burn at sunrise. Now, come drink her blood and get some rest. It's almost dawn." These words could be a scene from *Interview with the Vampire*. As long as you play the scene with believability and commit to this more bizarre scenario, these words also become a believable choice. I could tag the following on to that last bizarre line, "What's that? You are red cell intolerant and would prefer grape juice? Fine." It's a silly choice but still believable if played truthfully.

Less experienced improvisers may not have grasped that everything in improv, even the slightly off-center concepts in the scene, must be played truthfully and reacted as though serious in tone. It's imperative that both scene partners understand is and that in the world of the scene, even the strange things that happen must be taken seriously.

When you make believable choices, the scene will benefit, your character will benefit, and the spirit of the story will benefit. Even the simplest believable choices add to the strength of the scene, just as doing so in life keeps us on an even keel. Frank Gorshin gave everything to the scene. His characters filled the screen and fed off of audience energy. That can be you. Claim it.

YOU ARE WHAT YOUR MIND EATS

"You are what your mind eats" is a saying I heard over and over throughout my childhood. Okay, so maybe it wasn't those exact words, but close to it. So much of the truth in improv is because so much of being an improviser is about what your mind takes in and digests, and spits back out when you get up on the improv stage.

When stepping into an improv scene or playing an improv game, you are using energy, events, characters, beliefs and knowledge that you've gathered in your everyday life-- of which you bring some version to the world of the scene. Improv scenes are an exchange of energy and feelings.

The more information from which you have to draw, the greater your state of improv play. Makes sense, right?! Great improvisers crave knowledge in all its incarnations. Great improvisers read, whether it's a magazine, comic book, poetry, literary fiction, history or the newspaper. Great improvisers also make it their business to know a little something about history. Nowadays it's easier than ever to google any time period or event in history and have some success retrieving the information. Aren't you the least bit curious about where you live or someplace you've visited? I live in Boca Raton, Florida which loosely translates to "mouth of the rat". Where did that come from?

In the world of today with all its craziness, the concept of you are what your mind eats, is more important than ever with regard to our everyday lives as well. Unfortunately, though, everything in our world isn't always upbeat and positive, as we all have challenges to overcome. In improv though, you get the privilege of creating a world instantaneously, and existing in that world. Using your improv comedy sensibilities, you can also see these challenges from a unique viewpoint. Your skewed view of life events for the benefit of the improv scene should be a viewpoint drenched in irony. Those challenges or life events, that don't seem the least bit humorous at the time, can be the crux of your funny in improv. Season your scenes with irony.

As an improviser, life is your stage and the more information you take in, the more richness of detail your scenes stand to showcase. Remember, great improvisers explore and digest the world! Great improvisers also watch movies, television and YouTube, go to see plays, and most importantly, they watch other people in restaurants, at the gym or at the office, taking mental notes of interesting habits, personality quirks and interactions between the people they observe. Think of yourself as a Sherlock Holmes-- always on the lookout for clues to the mysteries of life. Think about it. You, revealing the mysteries of life. How fun is that?!

My point is that all the information that you as a person gather, can be reformatted, examined or re-examined, and played with on the improv stage for maximum humor. First, you must be observant and find things to observe that are of interest you, and secondly, you must be open to sharing that which you've observed with your scene partner on stage. Improv isn't just about humor either-- it's about telling an interesting story. Remember your scenes don't have to be funny either.

Just living life can also fill your idea coffers with information for later use-- and often truth is stranger than fiction as I've noted below.

SXSW

I was in Austin, Texas for the SXSW music conference. My label was showcasing several rap artists. In preparation for their performance the following night, I drove to my artists' hotel in the evening to go over the next day's schedule. As I arrived at their hotel, I caught two of my guys headed down to the lobby with their bedding and pillows in hand. In shock I stopped them; "Where are you going?" They responded casually; "We're going to sleep in the lobby to give so and so privacy." I said, "What?! No you're not. This is a nice hotel and you can't sleep in the lobby." This was an Embassy Suites and taking your bedding to the lobby for a nap was not appropriate. My artists' retort was "Oh." As I walked into their room through the door, the house phone rang. One of the guys handed me the receiver. "Hello.

Mr. Philippi?" I was taken aback not expecting the call to be for me, "Yes?"

"This is the front desk." "Okay." I was still slightly off balance. "Your girls are here." "Huh? My girls?" "Your call-girls are here." I nearly dropped the phone. "My what?" "Your call-girls." "I didn't order any girls." At that point, one of the guys with the bedding who was now back in the room standing beside me, piped in; "Oh yeah, that was so and so, he thought you wouldn't mind. So, he ordered a couple girls under your name." "Under my name?" "He didn't think you'd mind." Now I was mad. "Well I do mind." Now I'm thinking that we are close to being thrown out of the hotel, plus, I'm about to be billed for some ladies I didn't order, and things are getting strange. The next night things continued to spiral out of control when two of my artists had a fist fight in the room and another missed a radio interview because he had gone to the mall to buy new pants.

Just from the above couple of paragraphs you have information to use in your improv scene work that gives you all the basic elements needed for an interesting scene. The scene can be played in many different ways. Think about your own lives. You may not have had anyone use your name to order sex workers, on top of which you were about to be billed for, but you've still got a story yearning to be told, and it's your story. So, file that information from your personal life away for later use. No matter how mundane you think your story is-- it can be presented uniquely. It's your job as an improviser to flavor the information.

Improvisers are communicators and have some working knowledge of different types of careers, hobbies, geographical locations and foods, because improvisers are interested in the study of people and learning about themselves-- the more so the better. So, let's get started with a challenge.

CHALLENGE
You are going to become more observant in your own life. Start with the small things. If you usually shower by washing under your arms

first, start by washing your face or your legs first. Change up your routine. If you drive a certain path to work-- try another. Observe yourself. What do you see? How does the change feel?

Be aware of colors you see and how you feel when you see them, or of sounds or smells. Go into a store that you normally wouldn't go into and explore. I might normally go into an electronics store but never a fabric store. So, I should take a walk into a fabric store. When you go to a new place you haven't checked out, what do you see? How does it affect you? What feelings do you have? Take mental notes. Locate a map of the world and pick a country you've never heard of, and research some facts about it. All these experiences will provide energy and ammunition for your improv scenes and successful game play. Don't stop there. Keep expanding and exploring. Research at least one new piece of information each day.

DISCOVER THE SCENE

Scenes should be discovered. When improvisers try to write the scene in their head the scene gets very plotty. A plotty scene is cumbersome and not fun to watch or to be a part of. If an improviser is stuck in their head, it's because that improviser is trying to control the scene-- either out of fear or because of ego. To discover the scene, look at events in your life. Rewind an event and look back at how it unfolded. There is a focal point for the action, which is affected by the improviser's motivations and then affected by those around the improviser and their motivations.

INVENTING A NEW SOUND

I'm in Kindergarten. The teacher is speaking and I'm not paying attention because I'm developing a new sound by putting my lips together like a super loud motorboat engine. It's a very special sound. Perhaps the sound makes me slobber just a bit but who cares because this is such a cool sound. There's a girl seated at the desk in front of me. I want to impress her with this new sound. I can't stop to tell her about the sound because the sound might change, or I might forget how to execute this wonderful sound. I've got this. At least I think I do. I tap the girl on the shoulder, and she turns around to face me at which point I'm sharing my new sound with her. It's this intense motorboat engine noise. This sound is so cool.

Without saying a word, the girl gets up from her desk and heads to the front of the room where she reports to the teacher that I've spit in her face. The next thing I know I'm being snatched from my seat and am headed to the Principal's office—with the teacher. I'm certain that my new sound hasn't gone over well. I want to explain to my teacher that the entire episode is a misunderstanding. Chances are slim to none. She won't let me get a word in.

The teacher just keeps asking why would I spit in a girl's face. I still remember the teacher going on and on. All I can see is her skirt and legs from just above the knees and that she's wearing high heels which click with each harried step. I never look up. I've been tried and am now headed for the execution. I'm innocent but no one asks to hear my story. I'm in big trouble.

The next day I don't want to go to school. My parents ask and I eventually tell them why. I avoid the teacher when I return to class, but the girl seated in front of me doesn't seem all that angry when I finally am allowed back in class a week or so later. After several days sitting outside the Principals office the receptionist sends me back to class. I've enjoyed the quiet sitting in front of her.

The story above started with me discovering a wonderful new sound that I eagerly chose to share. In the end, I paid a big price when my offer was misconstrued. Now I often think of those who'd been incarcerated wondering how many were innocent. In improv we often either miss gifts altogether or misunderstand them.

If the above tale was an improv scene— and that scene had been forced and not allowed to unfold and to be discovered, then chances are that scene might not have had richness in character development, and intricacies of story that make a great improv scene.

Your scene on stage should mirror everyday life. It should flow as an event in life would flow. Your scene on stage should appear to the audience as any event happening in your life or theirs appears in your life or theirs with one exception. If there is an unusual thing, action or way of doing something in the scene it must be justified and played honestly. It must not be seen or played in a jokey way.

H-TOWN SOUTH SIDE

Fast forward several years to an industrial business park on the south side of Houston, and a studio with a name long forgotten. H-town is Houston. Houston's rap scene in the 90s was the dirty south, third coast, gangsta rap game and the scene was hot. Artists with the cache of Ice Cube, who it was rumored was often in town to buy tracks for his records, were doing so on the down low, so others wouldn't know where their new tracks came from.

At the epicenter of the H-town rap scene, I was running a label and doing so on the fly as I learned on the street about H-town rap dynamics. The emphasis was on being real and being in the moment. In the rap game art imitated life. On Houston's south side, art was life, at least that was the case during my time in Houston. It was the rap game that gave hope to fresh faces on the hip-hop scene. All arrived hoping to make their dreams come true.

COMMITTED, PASSIONATE, BEING IN THE MOMENT
At dusk, cars pulled up outside the studio I was working in. Groups of young MCs congregated around each car in the parking lot awaiting their turn to freestyle over heavy back beats, pulsating bass and synth driven rhythm tracks. Sometimes there were 4 or 5 cars with tracks playing at the same time. Young MCs would crowd around each car. These young rappers were committed, passionate and in the moment.

Improvisers please read that last sentence again and again, and focus on those last few words: committed, passionate and being in the moment. Improvisers exuding those traits can surpass the work of more experienced improvisers because those are the traits that lead to success. On stage, audiences long to be in the presence of committed, passionate and in the moment improvisers. So do other improvisers. People in general want to be in the presence of committed, passionate, in the moment individuals. Three simple concepts that play equally well on stage and in your everyday life.

The music was magical during my time in H-town. I became a fixture at the south side studio we were working in and went unnoticed in the parking lot, wandering between the cars, soaking in the sounds and listening to the various MC's flow. Watching the crowds around those cars, that was how I envisioned doo-wop groups drawing crowds during the 50's, on street corners in Philly and New York. However, the scene wasn't all an artistic Valhalla. After dark, the area where we were working was dangerous, especially for an unarmed creature of the burbs, alone and on the wrong side of the tracks.

As the sun disappeared, my regimen was to gather the artist I was recording as well as the engineer, plus any additional musicians needed for the session, and then we'd disappear into the studio. When I say disappear into the studio, we'd lock ourselves behind three sets of doors in the back of the building and work into the night emerging around 2 or 3 A.M. when everyone else had gone. The first few nights I was nervous and unsure of what I might emerge from the studio to find-- like my car missing or worse, but there was never an issue, and I looked forward to my nights there.

As the story unfolds in improv, as it is discovered, the characters sprinkle hot sauce over the scene in the form of emotions and wants. Patterns emerge as the characters relate to one another. Patterns fed by emotions and wants are important to upping the stakes of the scene.

Now take a look at your everyday life. Scenes tend to unfold in much the same manner. Rewind your day. Take a close look. What did a scene during your day look like as it unfolded? How did it feel? When and/or how did the story change? Think what could you have done to add to the excitement or intensity of the action, or add to the stakes? The stakes are often intensified when characters that have strong wants or strong emotions enter or leave the scene.

THE CLAW TELLS HIS STORY

One afternoon, the Claw, self-proclaimed moniker for a third coast MC, sought my council. Unfortunately, I felt that the Claw wasn't a very talented rapper and I didn't have the heart to tell him. I valued my own appendages too much. Though I grew to like him, the Claw was a menacing figure that stood roughly 6' 3" with a metal arm and claw pinchers for a right hand. Backing me into a corner one afternoon outside the studio, the Claw told the tale of his missing arm.

I didn't ask for the story. He insisted on telling it. As he did, the more intense his story became, the louder and more frequently his metal pinchers snapped-- like a pair of hungry hedge clippers inching toward an errant twig. I knew I needed to act fast and was attempting to be quite the charmer as his hungry hedge clippers chomped away. There was an ominous tone in his voice that intensified as he leaned in while telling his tale. It was a personal story and I-- his audience of one. As the claw moved toward me, I backed up until I could back up no farther. I was finally within reach of his metal arm and up against a wall. At that point, he leaned forward one last time and at that point suddenly broke into verse, rapping one of his self- penned pieces. Damn, it was an impromptu audition. Visions of an ambulance ride to the emergency room faded. Relieved, I nodded in acceptance.

As the Claw rhymed, his bloodshot eyes became slits in the sunlight and sweat poured from his brow. The Claw was high, but I was spared. Though he'd never make my label's roster, the Claw was part of a community that, through music, were sharing their aspirations, hopes and dreams-- all longing to create and be a part of something positive. I was merely an outsider looking in. I wanted to be support- ive but to do so from a distance.

Improvisers must be flexible when discovering the scene. An impro- viser in the moment has the freedom to discover the scene and quickly turn with it in any direction, and to do so at the drop of a hat as the events of the scene demand.

How does an improviser make sure they're in the moment? You sur- render to the scene. When you surrender to the scene, you take in all that is happening around you in the scene, and make it part of you, and you at the same time, become part of it. Being in the moment requires trust. Trust in the scene, trust that you've done the work dur- ing rehearsal, trust that your scene partner has your back. Trust in your own instincts, and lastly, trust that you are the scene and the scene is you. At that point, discovering the scene becomes magical.

IMPROVISERS ARE STORY TELLERS

Scenes tell a story. The most interesting stories are built around relationships. The more interesting the relationship, the more interesting the story. Interesting characters are an important element in storytelling. Potential characters include everyone you see on the street. The choices are endless. Everyone has a story-- a unique story waiting to be shared.

Potential characters can also be characters you craft from bits of personality you've gleaned from friends, family, co-workers and actors you've seen on television or those you've read about in books. The choices are endless. Next, there is the setting, and any outside motivations or influences.

"Coupon!" The clerk announced loudly acknowledging the couple in front of his check out station. "You've got a coupon?! You get 10% off!" The young man excitedly emphasized his words stepping from behind the register. He repeated the coupon statement in a loud voice, all the while gesturing with his arms to the customers in front of him. I was next in line. I had to say something, "Man, I've never heard anyone get so enthusiastic about redeeming a coupon." The woman in front of me with her kids, turned in my direction. "It was great! Uh, wasn't it?" In improv terms my mind began calculating. Who was this young man and how could his story affect the scene? How might his statement affect interactive play with the next customer? And what element might someone add to enhance this story?

Half an hour before my arrival at the store, local news reported it was safe to get back out on the roads in South Florida following a hurricane threat. I was going stir crazy and needed to get out of the house. The threat of that hurricane had just passed. Sprouts, a specialty foods store, had just opened. So, there I was in line.

A young girl bagging groceries stopped in-between bags, looked up, and offered some conversation. "You know, I could maybe meet my future husband here. He might be in the checkout line!" She was all smiles as she continued chatting. "You never know who you're gonna meet in line at the grocery store. It makes life exciting." She repeated her wishful thought. The young man behind the register nearby, added, "I can do this all day long, I mean work right here. I get my energy from the energy of the people that come through my line. I don't have to use my own. I can work right off them. I've met some interesting people too." I was learning his story as well as hers, including who he was and what he had to offer to the scene. Stories are not only made up of characters and locations, but details and specificity play a role.

HOPI NATION MESA 1

My mind flashed back to a trip I took to visit the Hopi Nation. Hopi is located right in the middle of Navajo country, in northern Arizona, on three mesas aptly named Mesa One, Mesa Two and Mesa Three. Hopi as a tribe, hold much different customs and beliefs from the Navajo. I was on Mesa One, a dusty dirt covered adobe wasteland, but for a few mud brick buildings. Native American dancers were doing a traditional dance-- not usually open to those from the outside-- but today they were sharing. I walked into an adobe structure where a woman sat at a folding table. There was no other furniture, just a sign that read "guides". "I'd like to hire a guide to walk through the old city." A few minutes later I was on a walking tour of the oldest part of the mesa built in 900AD where only 7 elderly women were currently living and practicing the old ways. There was no running water or electricity in the old part of the city.

It was a quick tour and as my guide was going through the motions, I posed a question to her. "Who is the most interesting person you've ever met on one of these tours?" Without hesitation she answered "A shaman (medicine man) from Africa. He traveled here from across the globe and took the tour barefoot wrapped in a single piece of ceremonial cloth. Yes, he was definitely the most interesting." Then I asked, "And have you ever *experienced* any UFO activity out here?" Looking off the Mesa I could see for hundreds of miles that there was nothing but more desert. "Yes" She paused a few seconds before continuing, "We were hunting in the desert and a disc-like craft flew in close. The craft was silently mirroring our movements. It continued to follow us, and we became scared, quickly making our way back to the Mesa. Then it flew off."

Everyone has a story. I was fascinated with hers. I had gained bits and pieces unique to her experience. Even though what I learned wasn't about her eating habits or relationships per se, I had learned first-hand -- that she carries emotions and memories experienced first-hand, and of interest to so many. All are part of the human soup we're all swirling about in. That soup being a mix of traits and habits, thought patterns, opinions and beliefs. Some are from our upbringing, some from experiences. All make us who we are today. Even our dreams are a part of who we are.

So that person standing by you in line-- what's their story? Who are they, really? Just realizing that everyone has a unique story is a great start for your improv.

I once met a woman in the nut aisle at Trader Joe's. She was getting ingredients for another man's dinner, and we ended up living together. Some might say meeting her in the nut aisle was a sign. Our interaction was part of her story and part of mine. It would have made a wonderful improv scene. In improv, we turn character interaction into stories and watch the chemistry between scene partners play out in varying scenarios.

Who's that person you are standing next to in the popcorn line at the movies? They might be dressed shabby but perhaps they've been working a month of 15-hour days, directing the latest blockbuster film, and haven't bothered to shave or change clothes. It happens in Los Angeles. It could happen anywhere. Multi-millionaire Howard Hughes was known to often wander around the seedy parts of San Pedro near the Los Angeles ship harbor, popping into tired seaside haunts, dressed in a dirty wrinkled suit, ordering a drink and producing wads of cash.

So what if they were homeless. Even the lowliest beggar has a tale to tell. In NYC I would often stop by Washington Square Park and sit with the homeless. There was one gentleman who'd be seated on a bench, reading *The Wall Street Journal* or leafing through a well-read *New York Times*. He'd help himself to cigarette butts on the ground. One day I struck up a conversation and learned he was a former executive and had been running an air freight shipping company. He was well educated and had fallen onto hard times. Those few details were just a sliver of his story. Other times, while at NYU, I'd brown bag it, taking a seat on the curb with the homeless. Of course, I'm not recommending everyone follow that advice.

The other day I walked into a Whole Foods. The cashier had a skateboarding ball cap. I asked him about it and if he skated. He said he liked the California skater lifestyle but could never skate because he didn't want to risk hurting himself. Then he explained that he's a professional MMA Wrestler. I was impressed. I looked up his bio and he had an impressive record of wins. He was very polite, but I sensed an edge just under the surface-- perhaps it was anger or rage. Think of what a character like that would add to a scene.

CHALLENGE
Go to a public place like the park, the mall, a school, an office, a restaurant, etc. Choose five people. Take out your notebook and for each of the five, write several descriptive paragraphs giving them traits that you deduce from how they move, speak, dress and/or interact with others. Take this challenge one step further. Choose five individuals you don't know and chat with them in a public place to get bits of their personality. Based on your deductions, craft them as characters on a sheet of paper. What is their story? How might their unique story affect a scene?

Be a storyteller on stage. Use bits of what you've observed in your daily life, share details, build relationships, introduce rich layered characters and make emotional connections in interesting locations.

LISTENING

One of the most important concepts in improv is listening. There are degrees of listening in improv--from hearing some of what has been said, to hearing all the words that have been spoken, to hearing the attached emotion the words carry. Active listening goes even farther. Active listening takes in every part of the person or situation you are listening to. You actually "hear" from facial expressions, body language, as well as vocal tone. Your gut comes into play as well. What is it telling you?

"Listen up!" Those were the first two and the last two words I remember our guide saying. I was definitely not listening. My mind was focused on the snow. I mean heck, there we were, standing on a mountain in Northern Colorado, where behind us, the snow was piled high-- I mean really high. I thought to myself, "Now *that* is a snow drift." It was like 15-20 feet high, maybe higher. I'd never seen snow so high. I was captivated and had to get some pictures. I got out my phone and began to snap a few. I didn't hear the guide say anything after "listen up" that is until he stopped his talk to the group and directed his attention right at me-- so he could bring me back into the fold. The guide was irked that I hadn't been listening-- I could hear it in his voice…He was former military. That was my first clue that I was in trouble.

Successful improv scenes require listening. In long form improv, the entire team should be focused in and listening for details to be utilized later and/or the establishment of a game. If you don't listen in long form improv chances are you are going to let down your teammates. Acting is reacting, but improv is listening and supporting your scene partner by responding directly to what was said honestly and with emotion. Improvisers should be able to hear the emotional intent that the words carry, and that's done by listening to the emotion traveling with the words. It's part of active listening--listening with your entire body and using all your senses.

Sometimes you may think you're listening when you are either only partially listening or not paying attention at all. Grownups do this all the time. Especially at parties. In either case you will pay a price, as I did in Northern Colorado, as you will read, continuing on. So listen up improvisers!

DOG SLEDDING IN THE ROCKIES
Northern Colorado after a heavy snow is beautiful. It's also quite cold. I don't ski, so dog sledding seemed like it might be an interesting option to fill an afternoon. I can tell you now, dog sledding is not as easy as you might think. The brochure did say it would be an adventure-- and it was. After a van ride to a remote site, a group of newly minted dog mushers gathered for a briefing before taking a three-hour mountain sledding trek. I was among them. This takes us back to the beginning of my Colorado adventure, when I made my first mistake and wandered away from the group-- albeit briefly to marvel at that towering snow drift which I described above. Hey, are you listening now? I wasn't then.

I was standing, mesmerized, by the tall snow drifts that stood like mountains to the side of our location. Our guide and head musher was an ex-military Drill Sargent and racing trainer, who I might add, still thought he was in the Marines, while he was going over basic sledding protocol. When my attention was finally pulled back, away from the snow mountain, the guide had stopped his talk to address me personally as everyone about to take this dog sledding adventure looked on. "Oh crap! That's never a good sign," I thought. I didn't think I had missed any pertinent info, but the former career military officer got a hair up his back side for my insubordinate action. I'd been taking photos during his talk. I had a feeling this ride was about to get bumpy.

I'd broken an important improv rule. I was not listening. I wasn't paying any attention to the people in my surroundings either. I wasn't reading the room, checking the energy, looking for clues about my potential scene partner's character. I should've seen that the instructor was ex-military and had a large ego. I should have known I'd needle him. Damn it-- I wasn't focused.

If you have ever done a scene without focus, it's always a disaster. I have done it-- I'm going in one direction and my scene partner in another and neither of us are listening. It's not any fun doing a scene when one or both scene partners are not listening.

Back on the mountain, the snow-covered cold mountain, we all had lined up awaiting our dog team assignments. The well-trained canines were several steps away and hooked to sleds. They seemed to calmly await their driver assignments. I caught a twinkle in our leader's eye as he caught my gaze for a second before returning to his list. He then called my name first, pointing to a specific dog team. I knew then I was in trouble. Damn it. He chose me first. Crap! The head musher had either assigned me the hounds from hell or a really sluggish team that would lag behind the others. There were a lot of us in the group and he singled me out.

As soon as the expedition started, I was in trouble. My dog team threw me into the first tall snowbank we passed, as we rounded that first curb. I pulled myself out of the snow and as I approached my sled, my dog team continued on without me. I ran after them in the deep snow, which was practically up to my thighs.

Yep, I had been assigned the hounds from hell! Out of breath, red in the face and breathing heavily, I was thrown from the sleigh a second time at another turn. Once again, just as I caught back up to the sled, and attempted to grab the reigns, the team took off, and ran down a steep embankment. I was almost dropped into a mostly frozen creek, and for the pièce de résistance of the ride, I was nearly pulled over the side of a cliff by my dog team. Ha! The view was both incredible- - and horrifying at the same time.

My wife had been riding on the sled under a blanket. It was at that point I switched places with her, being that I was drenched and covered with crusted ice, my skin was flushed, and my heart was racing. I could barely catch my breath. She now drove the demon canines on their hellish ride and like in the chariot races of old they'd eventually throw her. She was a brave soul.

Positioning myself on the sleigh I lay prone in the center, only a few feet from the dog's backsides, with a blanket pulled up to my chin, trying to stay as low as possible, while the team performed.

You see, these racing dogs perform at top speed and are fed a high protein diet which causes them to poop and have constant wind as they run, and my face was at butt level. These dogs were true competitors, much faster than the other teams, and the faster they ran, the more they farted and pooped. I had to constantly duck, hiding my head from flying feces, with my mouth clamped shut, as we raced across the slopes, and at times, teetered on the precipice.

I was paying the price for not listening earlier, and would continue to do so, for hours. I was not only paying the price, but so was my wife who was an innocent bystander. In an improv scene, if one scene partner is not listening-- both suffer.

As we came within several feet of the next cliff, my heart was beating even faster. I wondered if the sledding expedition company had good insurance. It wouldn't matter if I was dead. Our guide didn't seem to care. My wife who'd taken over driving the sled was now being dragged behind it. She barely hung on. My asthma kicked in and I was too weak to take over. I just kept my mouth shut-- tightly…One could easily state that this was the experience of a lifetime-- but not necessarily in a good way.

When the ride was over, my wife gave the owner a piece of her mind. Another couple on the journey with us laughed on the van ride back to our ski chateau. They continued laughing all night and into the next day. All because I hadn't been listening. It had been an adventure, and we'd survived. It wouldn't have been so funny had I gone off the cliff. Note to self-- in the future, listen!

JUST HEARING THE WORDS ISN'T ENOUGH
In improv, listening is the most important skill an Improviser can acquire-- and it is a skill. Just hearing words that were said is not enough. Improvisers are called on to process what they're hearing, and yet many improvisers are so hell bent on getting their viewpoint or the ideas in their heads out, that they don't even hear what's been said in the scene. The first level of listening in improv is to hear what's being said, process the words and then to respond to the words. That's only the first level.

As grown-ups, society tells us that listening is a fleeting thing that we only need to do with casual abandon. In normal conversation at a party, grown-ups only hear part of what is being said to them. Grown-ups at a party tend to hear subjects that we want to talk about, rather than what's been said. Improv not only calls for us to hear what's been said, but calls for active listening, which translates to listening with all your senses.

Seasoned improvisers don't think about how they should respond or what direction they might take the scene in when they listen. Seasoned improvisers respond directly to what has been said. Seasoned improvisers often look beyond the words-- detecting what emotion is being conveyed with those words. Seasoned improvisers deduce the emotion carrying the words by listening to voice tone, timbre, body movement, facial expressions and deciphering what is in their scene partner's eyes.

IMPROVE YOUR LISTENING SKILLS
How can you improve your listening skills? I'm glad you asked. There are of course improv exercises that help us focus on listening. Scene work also helps our listening.

In our daily lives there are everyday experiences that can help hone our listening skills. If you were working in an upscale men's wear store, and a man came in and said he wanted a new gray designer suit, first you might check to see if you have his size on the rack in the specific designer brand he's mentioned. However, if you were listening closely, you may have deciphered that the man has other clothing needs that he's not articulating, because he hasn't determined what those needs are. He may think he needs a gray sport coat when he should actually get a black Italian jacket which would be more appropriate for his board meeting or would coordinate better with items in his closet.

There could be many factors that affect his actual needs. He may not be familiar with newer designer names or maybe he hasn't bought a sport coat in quite some time so he's not sure what's available or which brands fit his body type best. Therefore, he's just asking for what he thinks he needs, but is unable to clearly ask for what he really needs. By asking the right questions, and listening, you can determine his true needs.

CHALLENGE
Take one day out of the week and make it the day from sunup to sundown focusing on listening to what others say to you--give listening your total focus. So, when someone speaks to you at the office or in a restaurant-- really hear them. About halfway through your day, listen not only to what is being said to you, but to what emotions their words carry. In some instances, the emotion attached to the words is very clear, and in other instances not so much. You'll find that by sundown, truly listening is hard work. Rewind the day. How was this day different from other days?

BE IN THE MOMENT

How present are you? As an improviser, being in the moment is all the ammunition you'll need to discover the scene. Being in the moment allows you to be spontaneous and connected with your scene partner at the same time.

Being in the moment-- this topic came to me as I was eating dinner at home, intending to write about it right after dinner. In the meantime, I got totally immersed in deciding what movie I was going to watch later that evening. Then, when I sat to write my topic, I couldn't remember what it was. During my dinner moment, I'd been so focused on what movie I was going to watch later that evening that I lost track of my thought that I'd had in the moment-- which was to write about being in the moment. I was thinking about the future when I should have been present in the moment. While looking ahead, I wasn't in the now, here, present. BEING PRESENT intersects with all other improv concepts.

You cannot be a successful improviser or have a successful scene unless you are in the moment. It's an important over-arching improv concept. So how can you rest assured you are in the moment? Anchor yourself in the scene, have an opinion about your scene partner, connect with them, then be ready for anything. Just be present. Had I been in the moment above, I'd have been present in the now and not reminiscing nor looking ahead to plan my evening. If I'd been in the moment, I'd have not known whether it was a past-present or future moment because I would have been living life at that moment and time would not have come to mind.

THERE'S A GUN IN MY CHEST

I pulled into the underground parking garage at my L.A. apartment, after brunch with a female friend. The morning had been pleasant and was still on my mind as I pulled into my parking spot. I opened the car door and found myself facing a man with a 9mm handgun, which he subsequently stuck in my chest demanding all my money. Damn, I didn't see that coming. Good thing I'd cashed a check the day before and had some cash. How could this happen? I thought I was more aware than that. Hadn't I been in the moment? Hardly. My mind was focused on the pastries and coffee and pleasant conversation I'd just enjoyed, as well as the woman I'd been enjoying them with. Therefore, I was in the past, NOT in the moment. I was not seeing the danger that was right before my eyes.

I'd missed so many signs. Later I would rewind the events of that day to find that if I had been in the moment, I'd have noticed the car with no plates pull up behind me. I'd also have noticed that same car follows my car through the security gate into the garage. Then I'd have noticed the car's occupant get out to approach my car with a gun in his hand. That day I was not in the moment. I missed so much. Sure, it was broad daylight-- but we were alone in that garage. As I put my hands on the wheel to show I was no threat, he was deciding whether to kill me. All this because I was not in the moment. I screwed up. I'll tell you one thing, now I *was* in the moment!

Sometimes we trick ourselves into thinking we're smarter and more aware than we really are, and that we're focused and listening, when in fact we're not. We often lull ourselves into a false security to convince ourselves that we're tuned into our surroundings. Still old habits die slowly. I didn't get the lesson.

As adults, we multi-task, and in doing so, we take in a part of several things that are happening at the same time. You might be chatting with a co-worker by the coffee machine while partially listening to another co-worker discuss a project that you're also working on, while pouring some coffee, and attempting to add a specific amount of artificial sweetener. The truth is-- you are not fully present in either of the three activities. Be in the moment. Be present. Old habits die hard. So…

SECOND TIME IS THE CHARM
I was robbed at gun point a second time. WTF?! Huh? Dumb, right? Wrong place, wrong time? Maybe. I couldn't help thinking that there must be a life lesson for me in there somewhere. I was unfocused

and unaware and far from being in the now. Let's rewind this particular evening's events.

I was walking down a side street in Los Angeles, a dark side street late into the evening. A car flew around the corner and pulled up onto the curb. The door flew open to reveal an angry gangsta' with his 9mm handgun pointed at my torso. Crap! Again?! Damn...

The gun toting gang member was yelling obscenities that only got worse when I offered my pizza box with 2 leftover slices. Bad move. I'm a comedian but what was I thinking? That was my ironic view of life. The lightness of my suggestion wasn't appreciated.

I hadn't been paying attention. I'd checked out. It was late and I wasn't aware of my surroundings. Maybe I was trying to make up for not being in the moment by saying something with a skewed viewpoint, or maybe I was just nervous. Now I was in the moment and was thinking: tomorrow's headlines could read **Unknown Comedian Dies in a Hail of Gunfire**. That headline didn't sit well with me. I was in a bad situation and I was there because I hadn't been in the moment.

To be present is a simple skill. Yet we complicate it because our minds have the ability to wander, and grown-ups, overall, lack the focus to be and stay in the moment. As adults we want to look ahead rather than just be. As an improviser, sometimes you need to plant yourself in the scene and just be. As an improviser, you must train your mind to block out ego in its many forms, so you can be present in the scene. Ego is telling you to check your phone or that you are hungry or to do something to get people's attention, such as: I'm kinda hungry, I like his shoes, etc., instead of taking in all that is around you— the people, places, things and what's going on between them. Being in the moment is a skill, that when practiced enough, becomes a good habit. A powerful positive habit.

Being in the moment is anchored in the art of listening. Being in the moment will make it easier for you to have your mind in the scene and on your scene partner, and easier to support your team members, digest details outside your body and to look for creative themes to extract and act on-- all at the same time. Being in the moment keeps you in the game. Take a breath, clear your mind and anchor yourself in the moment. Hear and feel only the scene and your scene partner. Shut out ego!

CHALLENGE

Find a scene partner. Focus inward. When a thought comes into your mind do not focus on the thought or explore it but clear it away. Erase any thoughts that try to sneak in. Keep clearing all thoughts away until you have a blank slate. Visualize a blank slate. Visualize nothingness. Tell yourself nothingness. I use either a black space or a white space and visualize it with nothing. Allow no thoughts, see no words, no pictures-- just nothingness. You are clearing out all the debris in your mind. This should only take a minute or two max. Your ego will try to fight back, to trick you into letting your mind wander.

Once you have a blank slate, then open your eyes and make a statement to your scene partner who is standing in front of you. Any statement that is short and personal will do. Say the statement again but attach a feeling to your statement. When your scene partner answers you with a short statement, hear only their words and the emotion attached to those words.

If their response does not directly connect with what you've said, call them on it. "Mark, you're always copying my homework. I can't get caught cheating so stop it. I need a scholarship, or I won't get to go to college." If Mark's response is unrelated as though he wasn't listening, such as, "Your mom sure makes great cookies," call your scene partner out for ignoring you. I guarantee the audience is doing so in their mind. Bob might pull Mark back in with something like, "Just because the test is tomorrow doesn't mean you can ignore my statement Mark!"

After 3 or 4 lines of dialogue, stop and repeat the exercise. Rewind what just happened in your mind. Were you in the moment? Try adding an improvised action like making breakfast while you are interacting with your scene partner and repeat the exercise. Are you still in the moment? Did the movement (object work in improv) hinder or help your connection with your scene partner?

Be in the moment, and always expect the unexpected-- because it's coming, that unexpected thing-- the one you are not ready for.

PASSION

When I think about improv, I think about what speaks to me about the craft. Ultimately, it's my passion for expression and connecting with others on stage that attracts me to improv. For some, passion and being passionate translates to volume and over the top intensity, but for me, it's something that stirs my soul--a quiet intensity.

What has drawn you to improv? Stress relief? Laughter? Is it a form of therapy? Perhaps you're exploring self? Maybe all the above. Perhaps other points? Sometimes it's good to take a minute, step back and take stock of how we define passion and examine where our passions lie.

DAD, FISHING, AND THE WOLFMAN

Dad was listening to Wolfman Jack as we drove off into the night toward our deep-sea adventure. The Wolfman was a legendary DJ whose career started on the underground circuit broadcasting illegally, but later he became a household name following his appearance in the George Lucas film *American Graffiti* and then appearing on network television as a live music host.

Nothing put a smile on my dad's face faster than deep sea fishing, and we were on our way. It was his passion. As a young boy, I remember dad driving me up the coast, a couple of hours north of Los Angeles, to board an overnight fishing boat that would take us beyond the Channel Islands to the deep waters of open sea. Around midnight we'd arrive, board the boat, find a bunk and go to sleep below deck. The next morning we'd awaken at our first location, far out at sea, unless rough waters woke us earlier.

On this particular trip, Wolfman Jack blared from the car's radio. The Wolfman was the gritty hyped-up soulful voice on radio XERB, a powerful soul station broadcasting from Mexico. XERB was pumping out 250,000 watts of power which happened to be 5x the legal limit of American stations, enabling the Wolfman's show to be heard throughout much of the U.S.

There was a hint of danger in his voice as though we were listening to forbidden commentary on the down low. Hot R&B tunes and the Wolfman's risqué banter with call-in listeners were both entertaining and eye opening for a young boy. Wolfman Jack would become a pop culture icon, a television icon, and thus fenced in by the medium. His days on the radio however had no boundaries and were sometimes quite wild. He'd riff on a theme in a stream of consciousness all virtually improvised and designed to push boundaries. Occasionally too far. However, Wolfman Jack wasn't an overnight sensation.

Wolfman Jack exuded passion. He was intense, overly enthusiastic, and practically a caricature of himself on the big or little screen. It wasn't so much his volume, but his actions that showed his passion for life. The Wolfman brought energy to anything and everything he worked on. He wasn't always a commercial success though. He struggled and he tasted life. He had passion for the world of entertainment, and he never let that passion go.

Before turning to the mic as a DJ, Wolfman Jack tried his hand at singing R&B himself, as well as hosting interracial dances in northern Louisiana, which resulted in the Klan burning crosses both in front of the club and on his own front lawn. That didn't stop the Wolfman. He was a larger than life character-- so filled with passion that it spilled over into everything he did--passion that sometimes put him on the wrong side of the censors. As an artist and later as a DJ, the Wolfman sometimes impaled himself on his own passion, though never any career ending moves. The Wolfman was testing the waters, feeling out the parameters on the stage, and often stepping over boundaries by accident or seeing what he could get away with.

His story as a public figure is evidence for the existence of passion, which lives within us all. If there's no passion, is life worth living? The reason I'm even writing about passion is because passion is an integral part of improv, as it is in life, and the subject gets little attention.

WHAT'S IN YOUR HEART?

Passion drives great characters and cements relationships on stage and off. Fishing was my father's passion. Dad never really went overboard with his passion except one time when we were scheduled for a deep-sea fishing trip. No boats were leaving the harbor because of rough storm seas. We found a Captain willing to go out when no other boats would. As we made our way past the Channel Islands off Santa Barbara, the seas got increasingly rough. Soon there were 30 foot or larger swells, and no one could fish. We nearly capsized twice. That's when the Captain opted to return to port. For hours, my legs were still at sea. The Captain had a passion for the sea, or he would not have gone out that day.

PASSION OR NO PASSION

The average improviser doesn't show enough passion in their work. They are either afraid to act passionately because they're worried about what others think or they haven't figured out how to focus that passion. Does passion really need to be focused? Can it be? Probably not. Passion just is. It's intense and uncontrollable. In improv it's all about show, don't tell. Actions speak louder than words. Show your scene partner and the audience more passion. In turn, your commitment level will increase.

While most improvisers have plenty of room to bring up their passion levels, some are over the top. They've managed to pin the passion meter in the red. If you're out there you know who you are! I can be too mellow, or I can be one of those. Take stock and if you're too passionate on stage dial it back and avoid impaling yourself on your own passion on stage. If you need to dial in more passion, then be prepared to do that by checking in with yourself and tapping into how you feel. When in doubt about what to say—think, how do you feel?

An actor who has done quite a bit of stage work gets called in for a network television audition. The casting director stops the actor during his reading and gives him an adjustment, explaining that the actor is being too theatrical. Too theatrical is too intense, too over the top.

The casting director is asking the actor to dial his performance back a notch or two.

How do you know when you've taken your passion beyond the barriers? First, let's find the passion, define what passion is for you, then test the waters. Start by thinking what is it in your life that stirs feelings deep in your gut-- feelings that move you to act. Think what subject(s) you can just talk and talk about without being prompted. What makes you feel whole? I'm certain you'll discover that the answer is something you're passionate about.

Your passion is part of who you are as an improviser. Improvisers constantly must dial up or dial back their performances. It's part of being an improviser and being flexible. More often than not your performance can use more passion.

Wolfman Jack found his voice, his style and the approach to his craft, through sheer passion. The best characters an improviser can choose to play are strong characters, because they are characters that require commitment and to be played truthfully. Add passion to your scenes to give them a sense of urgency!

Wolfman Jack was at times impaled by his own passion. He forgot boundaries and stepped over the line. For those few improvisers who occasionally get too passionate, there's the risk of passionate impalement. It's not common but it does happen.

PASSIONATE IMPALEMENT
Passionate impalement is committing improv hari-kari. Ask yourself, is committing improv hari-kari really honorable? In simple terms what you're doing is acting passionately in a situation yet forgetting the parameters you are working within. It's as though you're falling on your own sword, but not in an honorable way. This is improv so at least do it with a dramatic flair.

As an improviser playing with an overabundance of passion you are wielding a double-edge sword. When there's a double-edge sword at work, it's going to cut both ways and the scene is going to bleed. Passion is an important element of play in improv. You do not want to leave out passion, but you don't want to over play either because your character then becomes a caricature of itself. When I teach classes, I have to beg most improvisers to put more passion into their scenes. Perhaps they're afraid that if they show passion, they'll be vulnerable. However, improv is about vulnerability. That's why I attempt to create a safe space in my classes so that improvisers can feel comfortable trying new things and being vulnerable. A great way to measure how much passion to put into any scene is for you to hold the scene in your heart! The heart never lies.

PASSION IN LIFE

The Universal Amphitheater Hollywood concert hall (1972-2013) had no roof for years. The usually dry, tepid, though sometimes cool evenings in southern California made shows under the stars a wonderful experience. I was working the venue in the evenings as a second job.

The best part of the job was addressing the ticket holders as they streamed through the gates before the show, sharing rules and regulations such as restroom locations and where sections are located. I'd use a megaphone to speak with the crowds. I found the challenge of delivering **clear** and concise information rewarding, by doing so in varying accents and dialects, and sometimes as the characters that use those varying accents and dialects.

The crowds loved it. They ate it up. So much so that I tried to cover multiple entrance areas in a short time, reaching as many concert goers as possible. One evening I was even able to seat Brian May of Queen for a Sinatra show. He was more interested in finding a seat than my clever banter since he was late, but Brian was a gentleman.

Though the crowds devoured my repartee, my supervisor, well…not so much. I was verbally reprimanded and then eventually suspended. I'd allowed the lines between the world of our daily lives and the world of the scene to be blurred by my passion. I was overly passionate, impaling myself on that passion. This doesn't happen often because so many improvisers are lacking in the passion department but in this case, I'd gone overboard, I went a little too far…Yes, I carried out all the duties of the job BUT I went beyond, in areas that rankled management. Know your boundaries. At least be prepared to pay the price if you know you might overstep.

I should have been more aware. Maybe I was, subconsciously. Consciously however, I suffered. My passion was too great, and I went overboard and paid the price. Most improvisers will never have the problem of being too passionate. That space is reserved for a select few. If you are one of those folks, you are not alone…Wolfman Jack, remember him? He was a bit overly passionate at times but the Wolfman learned to focus his passion and used it to his advantage. You can harness and focus your passion. You're an improviser. How do you feel? Now add some passion.

PASSION TO DO THE WORK

In every arts discipline, and improv is no exception, you have put in time doing the work to get results. Doing the work with regard to improv is putting in the time to learn the unwritten rules of improv and applying them.

In improv to do the work you must first have a passion for the craft. My passion for improv drives my wanting to teach, perform and watch improv. If you don't have a passion for improv you won't do the work, and if you don't do the work, your creativity will not be fully realized. You can be an improviser that doesn't have a passion for the craft and that's fine-- but why do anything half-way? Make the mental connection with the craft to go all in, and your work will be far above what it might have otherwise been. Do you have a passion for the craft? Check in with yourself. Ask yourself, how do you feel? Then ask yourself what's in my heart?!

COMMITMENT

Commitment is a concept that says you, the improviser, are dedicated to a cause, an activity or a concept in the scene. As an obligation or commitment can restrict freedom of action, it takes a strong-willed improviser to commit. At the same time, commitment keeps the improviser focused and within the parameters of the scene. Commitment goes hand in glove with passion.

Passion is a strong and at times barely controllable emotion. Improvisers with passion are exciting to watch. However, it's when you couple the magnetism of passion with the driving force of commitment that your improv will seem more focused and reach new levels. Coupling the two makes your state of play fresh, exciting and edgy. Commitment is your obligation to a craft you are passionate about. Passion is the raw emotion that craft delivers.

Great improvisers commit to the scene, their character, the premise, or the game, once the premise has been established. Commitment showcases a strong belief system. An improviser committed to the scene does not appear indecisive on stage no matter what their choices are. Without commitment the characters and the scene itself both play flat and unexciting.

Punk rock and the New York City underbelly--life doesn't get more passionate than that! When I was pursuing a career in music, my work as a guitarist in the punk scene in New York City was filled with passion. Making a commitment to realizing my passion and pursuing my musical dreams, gave my journey a framework that kept me focused, and away from the unsavory elements of the scene.

What are elements of commitment in your life? Transport those elements to the stage. Allow them to live through your art. A scene without commitment is unrewarding. A life without commitment is one that is adrift. When you commit to something or someone, you believe in it, or them. If you slip, refocus and recommit. Commit to yourself-- to being a better you in life, on stage and in class.

SETTING THE SCENE

In 1979, *Daily Variety* touted my band, US Ape, as the new Blondie. I was the guitarist. Blondie had just been signed to Chrysalis Records and were making headlines and about to dominate the charts. An executive from Chrysalis had come to see my band at Max's Kansas City, a hip, mid-town Manhattan club. Max's was the club where artist Andy Warhol often held court in the restaurant downstairs, with the Velvet Underground and other New York scenesters.

My band, US Ape, was more punk than pop, and on the cusp of fame and fortune-- or so we thought. US Ape had been written up in the trades and we'd opened for numerous signed, touring punk acts plus we were starting to headline ourselves. However, infighting had already begun taking a toll. We were all just keeping our heads above water financially, but our spirit on stage and off was high. We were determined. I was graduating from NYU and needed a place to live if I were to stay in the city. So, I began my search. The streets of Manhattan were dangerous in 1979 but I didn't see it as a deterrent. We were seduced by the music and the scene. Passion and commitment kept the band moving forward though by September of that year, there were over 250 felonies on the subway every week. NYC had the highest crime rate for any mass transit network in the world.

I realized squabbling among band members was getting out of hand when I got an urge to punch the bass player on stage at a sold-out show. Arguments should be resolved by one of the two arguing to propose a compromise or walk away and not to end the argument physically. The same goes for improv. On stage the sensible solution is that one of the scene partners must give up and be willing to lose the argument. If no one does, the scene becomes an unwatchable mess that makes the audience cringe. Where's the funny in that?

When one of the scene partners is willing to lose the argument, the character relationships in the scene move forward-- thus moving the scene forward. Remember, when your scene partner looks good you look good! Always make your scene partner look good.

40

Our rehearsal spot was a grimy mid-Manhattan basement, where roaches the size of rodents waddled across the floor. "It's a water-bug!" a band member would state matter of fact. "Can I saddle and ride it?" I'd ask. Moving equipment to-and-from gigs was a challenge. After gigs we'd lower our equipment back down into our rehearsal hole two levels below street level, squeezing it into a pass-through space, then down a bit deeper to its final destination. Our drummer slept there in our rehearsal space on a mattress on the floor by our gear. He invited me to join him. I was impressed that he was so com-mitted to the concept of our band he agreed to sleep with his gear and any number of visiting bugs. The room was damp, dark, unwel-coming not to mention the bugs. I passed. I was passionate and com-mitted to the music and our band, but I wasn't that desperate.

A month or so later, our drummer moved into a condemned building filled with unusual tenants. A new level of commitment? The theory was that someone paying something would keep squatters out, so officials allowed it. While the building's future was being decided, the rent was next to nothing. Our drummer invited me for a tour, and while doing so, tried to sell me on the building's amenities. There were none. Was I committed enough to the band to move in? There's com-mitment and then there's-- COMMITMENT! I wasn't so sure I was ready for that much commitment.

The building was a walk-up with skinny halls and tiny dorm room sized apartments. Tenants resembled the cast of a Star Wars film and included: recent parolees who posted their prison mug shots on their doors, at least one drug dealer, an odd dog owner with a dog large enough for a kid to ride that resembled *Scooby-Do*, and other colorful characters. This was Manhattan in the late 70s and the build-ing's tenants were pioneers in the belly of the beast.

To even consider living in such conditions meant I was committed to moving my career forward. Maybe I should have actually been com-mitted for considering taking up residence in a place that resembled the set of the film *Escape from New York*!

In improv, if you commit to the scene, you can be less trained than another improviser and hold your own or even outshine them, because commitment to the scene will carry your performance. Living in the drummer's building though, that was a step beyond commitment to any craft.

There was a bathroom at the end of the hall for all residents to share. It had a shower and toilet. The tile floor was questionable. Better not forget your shower sandals I thought. Moments before I arrived our drummer had evidently been robbed and was yelling down the hall for something to be returned. As I squeezed down the skinny corridors, I was taking it all in while at the same time I noticed how flimsy the individual apartment doors appeared.

"Ummm, what do you do for security?" I asked, kinda thinking out loud. He pulled a lead pipe out from under his bed. "It's my criminal deterrent" he replied. In improv, yelling down the hall while brandishing a lead pipe, "Return my stuff before I have to beat it out of you!" is more than commitment. Sure, it would be a short statement in a scene that demands an emotional response. Sure, making that short statement that demands an emotional response probably would result in stronger scenes, but this was life not an improv stage. The whole scenario was more commitment than I was ready for.

"Here's what I brought you over to see!" he said as we peeked into the room next to his. It was empty and ready for occupancy other than several piles of debris. "All this can be cleaned out plus we can just knock the wall through and make it a suite!" He chirped in a sales tone. I scanned the room trying to hold my contempt. "So how bad is the roach problem?" "Oh, I just brush them off and keep moving." That statement sealed my decision. Not to be too abrupt I said I'd think about it. It wouldn't make sense living in the city if all my music gear was stolen. This place wasn't safe let alone sanitary…

Commitment. It's a powerful word. Commitment says I believe in you and what you're doing. The question you must answer is, how committed are you to yourself? Believe in yourself, and your commitment level will define itself.

EMBRACE THE UNEXPECTED

Land Crabs and Michael Jackson-- two subjects that are seemingly unrelated though both crossed my path in unexpected events. Both took place as scenes in my everyday life though they could have been scenes on a stage. Note to self; Buckle up, your scene is about to get interesting, and it could be a bumpy ride! No these aren't the words of an announcer on a Disney ride. This is the world of the scene. Where the arrival of the unexpected can happen at any point. How many times have you stepped on stage to start an improv scene thinking, yes, I'm ready for anything but when the scene takes an unexpected turn, you are lost and left sucking air? That's when you should embrace the moment and hold on. Don't know what to say?! Regurgitate what your scene partner's just given you and have an opinion about it. The scene has the answer even if you, at the moment do not.

THE ELEMENT OF SURPRISE
Imagine my surprise when I awoke early one morning and stepped out my back door to be greeted by a large crab on the edge of my yard just off my porch in South Florida. It appeared to be a blue crab with large pinchers and was blowing bubbles as crabs do. Let me be clear, I do not live at the beach. Panic set in. I'm losing it, I thought. There's a large blue crab in the yard by my back porch. I ran back inside. I guess I should grab my shoes and a box so I can drive the crab several miles back to the beach! Those were my first thoughts, followed by thoughts of a dimensional space-time warp. The world raced through my brain like a freight train with no brakes-- spiraling down a mountain with no guard rail.

My brain's go-to cause for the crab's arrival, was that a freak storm sucking beach crabs into the sky and depositing them several miles inland, had happened in the night. I decided to splash some water on my face and throw on some jeans so I can scoop up the crab in question and drive it back down to the beach and the safety of salty coastal waters. I was trying to embrace the unexpected.

When I returned to the spot by my porch where I'd discovered the crab, with my shoes on and keys in hand, the crab was gone. No crab, no bubbles, no clues, and the trail had grown cold. Had it all been a dream? That's when I sat down at my computer to research the subject and staring back at me from my screen was the rare, protected, Blue Land Crab of Florida that travels up to two miles inland from the beach, where it lays its eggs. Wow! A creature of the sea traveling two miles inland and it choose my yard! Now that was unexpected.

EXPECT THE UNEXPECTED

How do we prepare for the unexpected? Can we prepare? Improv rehearsals are helpful. Let's take a deeper dive. Improv scenes, more often than not, have unexpected moments that are at times uncomfortable moments. The best way to prepare is to tell yourself to be ready for the unexpected. Be ready to first accept whatever comes your way, then feed some version of it back to your scene partner. Improvisers are taught to go with the flow of the scene, to flex, to follow the developments of the scene, and not write in their heads.

When the scene takes an unusual turn, sometimes all your performance prep goes out the window. When that happens, many improvisers either totally freeze or squirm a bit before being able to refocus provided they're able to get back on track. There are several causes for short circuiting when the unexpected comes to call. Often the scene partner who freezes is in their head instead of being in the moment. It's hard to react if you're not present. Other times the improviser who freezes is just not in sync with their scene partner. They have not been paying attention to the rhythm of the scene and are paying the price. .

If you're about to jump on stage and you observe a scene is moving quickly, just before you put yourself in that scene, speed up your thought process to match the action in the scene. Feel the rhythm before jumping in. If you do, you'll hear more acutely, you'll feel deeper and you'll be able to ride the scene because you're in sync with your scene partner. So, when they serve up the unexpected, it will be much harder for you to be thrown.

Every game and every scene have a rhythm. Life has a rhythm. Be aware of the pace around you. Once you're in the rhythm of the scene you can turn on your active listening. Start by feeling the impact of the words and the intent behind them.

MICHAEL JACKSON

I was in a comic bookstore and Michael Jackson walked in. Yes, he does walk like he dances! …or did… Michael kind of floats across the room. That day no one expected he would come into the comic store, therefore I found Michael Jackson's arrival to be an unexpected event. He had called the store to say he was a few blocks away and asked the store management to close, but the store was having a sale and said they couldn't. It was an unexpected event for the store.

When Michael entered the store, he made his way to the back, where I was shopping. Appearing almost choreographed, Michael was floating from point to point, gathering goods and piling them by the register. He's a fast shopper. In fifteen minutes, he'd racked up several thousand dollars' worth of merchandise. I on the other hand was attempting to nab a few cheap sale comics before someone else and kept one eye on the racks while watching Michael purchase big-ticket figurines and toys.

I turned and suddenly found myself a foot away from Michael's face, and in that moment, instead of asking him for an autograph, I asked Michael Jackson to please move over so I could see a particular comic. He was startled. I was startled. Seconds seemed like hours. It was an unexpected moment. "Uh, excuse me…" I said. "Yes?" (long pause) Michael had spun around and was looking directly at me. "Do you think I could check out that section?" "Oh sure." He said in a soft voice. We were less than a foot away from one another. I had asked Michael Jackson to step aside so I could get to a comic book! Why?!

It was especially unexpected moment for Michael Jackson. He wasn't quite sure how to respond at first. Michael had been ready for me to ask for an autograph, but I hadn't done so. That's why the long pause before Michael spoke. To be clear, it wasn't that I didn't respect or appreciate Michael Jackson's talent either. I was just trying to treat Michael Jackson like anyone else and respect his privacy. I also was dealing with the unexpected and probably should have gotten the autograph.

When Michael Jackson and I spoke, that was our scene. That's where we established our scenic rhythm. Michael had been moving all over the store and therefore he came into the scene with a fast rhythm which he had to slow slightly as his energy intersected with my slower energy. I'd been casually shopping. That point was the point of intersection for us. When he left, a store employee approached me. "Hey man, that was so cool the way you just treated him like a regular guy and didn't ask for an autograph." It was just an unexpected moment.

When the unexpected happens in improv, give thanks. Accept what you've been given, then try to add something and pass it back. If you tell yourself before the scene even starts that you are going to be getting something unexpected, and that you'll be fine it's easier to embrace the unexpected when it comes. Know this in your heart and answers will be given to you.

Remember, that scenes are personal, scenes must connect emotionally, and it's okay to let the unexpected throw your character off slightly. That's part of the truth of the scene. However, know that if you are in the rhythm of the scene, you'll find it easier to ride that horse. Brace yourself-- it's going to be a bumpy ride, but a heck of a lot of fun! Unexpected fun! Isn't that why you watch and play improv?

MAKE YOUR SCENE PARTNER LOOK GOOD

When you make your scene partner look good you look good. Play off the energy of others in your scene. Use it to connect with them positively or negatively. Think, "what action can I do to make my scene partner look good?"

When climbing the corporate ladder, it's often a challenge to balance making your boss look good while attempting to take credit for your actual accomplishments. You want your boss to look good, really good, but you don't want to get passed over because no one is seeing what you're doing. In life, it's a thankless job to make your scene partner look good in life.

I once embarrassed my wife in front of her Executive Leadership team. I'd been invited to speak in front of everyone and was using the space to be funny and engaging, but it was her team and I should have been making her look good. She was my scene partner. The key is to play off your scene partner's energy so that the scene is cohesive. In doing so, you are building an emotional bond with your scene partner while making them look good.

When both scene partners drive the energy of the scene, characters appear more dynamic. That same exchange of energy between the improvisers on stage gives the scene a playfulness. The trust shared in the scene adds an additional dynamic. Think: what can your character say that will make the character standing next to you appear brilliant? Not what can your character say or do to make *you* look brilliant-- at the other character's expense.

LOST IN THE SCENE? I'VE GOT YOUR BACK!
Sometimes we become lost in the action. At that point you can either panic on stage or play off the energy of your scene partner. Using clues from their actions, you can restart or reconnect yourself to the

scene. Sometimes just focusing on your scene partner is enough. Sometimes just knowing they are there for you if you falter, is enough. From time to time, support comes from the most unlikely place in the scene.

The Eagles' guitarist, Joe Walsh, was pacing in his dressing room at the House of Blues in Los Angeles, as we entered. The Artist Relations Manager for Gibson Guitars asked if I'd take some digital photos for promotion. I thought, sure, why not? Digital cameras had just been introduced. Phones didn't even have digital cameras yet, and I'd never even held a digital camera, let alone used one. The Artist Relations Manager handed me the digital camera outside Joe's dressing room, and I felt its sleek metal sides and rectangular shape. All I could think is, "It can't be that hard," and at the same time, "where is the on/off button?" Uh… I'm in Joe's dressing room and I don't know how to work this camera.

Joe was to pose for a couple of quick publicity shots that were to be instantly uploaded, emailed and posted on the Gibson Guitars site in Nashville. What's the big deal, right?! I know, it's a process we take for granted these days, but at that time, the whole process was new.

Joe had made his way to the couch there in the green room and was fiddling with something. He stopped what he was doing, got up off the couch and came over to us. Joe Walsh posed in front of me a few feet away. It was like he expected us and was saying, okay let's get this over.

In improv we often try to force the scene, assuming it should go in a particular direction or giving the scene a nudge to go in the direction we'd like it to go in. However, in time, the scene will answer all your questions, unfolding before you. Your job as an improviser is to be patient. Let it play out and in the interim look at specifics, important details, with the idea that you are going to use them to make your scene partner look good. That's why great improvisers don't just discover the scene. They bring the audience along with them on the journey. What better way to do so than to support your scene partner.

In doing so you guarantee their success, and in turn, your success as the story unfolds.

I'm standing in front of Joe Walsh thinking, "Uh this scene is going to implode. There will be nothing to discover. I'm about to make a fool of myself." "Take the picture!" the Artist Relations Manager is calling out. "I can't freakin' see him," I reply, followed by, "Uh, what do I push?" Remember, this is the dawn of digital photography and like a cave man, I'm clueless-- until I'm not. Joe makes a face. I glance at him from around the camera. I guess I have this look on my face that says, "I'm lost." It's an honest look.

Honesty wins the day. Joe Walsh is about to start laughing. "Is there a button?" I spout, then continue my ramblings. "Where is it? Does it make a sound? Do I need a flash? Dude, is the viewfinder indicative of what the photo will look like?" I am frustrated and want to throw the camera out the window or would have if there was a window. At this point I'm turning red with embarrassment. Then I stop, get hold of myself and look around the room. It's sink or swim time. Joe Walsh has the power to bury me. The Artist Relations Manager, a kind friend, does as well.

I'm thinking about improv. Before a show, the team will often get in a circle and everyone turns to the right to place their hands on the improviser's shoulders to their right, stating, "I got your back! I got your back!" The team members repeat this mantra over and over until it's burned into their brains. It's imperative that improvisers remember that if your scene partner knows you have their back, they'll be more apt to step out and take chances. They'll also be more apt to follow the unwritten improv rule-- "dare to fail"-- because your teammates know that someone else on the team will step up when needed. Your teammates will be more apt to save your ass when it needs saving, so that your light shines on stage!

Joe Walsh had my back that evening. He let me know everything would be okay. He made me feel at home and relaxed. It wasn't anything he said nor even anything he did. It was more of a knowing look, a chuckle and a smile. Joe had an attitude that spoke to me saying, "It's going to be okay. It's only a photo. I've got your back!" I've worked with numerous musicians and actors and some big stars. Joe Walsh could easily have crushed my ego, and embarrassed me, but he did not. On a personal note: If you're reading this and you're a rock fan, check out "The James Gang Rides Again," an album by the band Joe formed while at Kent State, The James Gang.

The Eagles have sold more than 150 million albums, were inducted into the Rock and Roll Hall of Fame, won a Kennedy Center Honor, 9 Grammy awards and 5 American Music Awards.

PLAY OFF OTHERS IN THE SCENE
My peripheral vision that night revealed the Eagles' bassist, Timothy B. Schmidt, to my side, watching us with a serious look on his face. I don't think he was enjoying the humorous scene unfolding before him. Thinking back, I'm glad I wasn't photographing him. I used his energy to play.

Farther back in the room, stood iconic rock photographer, Henry Diltz, who'd taken pictures of The Doors, Jimi Hendrix, Buffalo Springfield, Janis Joplin, CSNY, Neil Young, Michael Jackson, Frank Zappa, Queen, David Bowie and Apple founder Steve Jobs. Diltz was watching as well. Diltz had a look on his face that said that maybe, just maybe he should intervene, but my own Spidey sense told me that Diltz hadn't made the move to digital yet. I was, after all, holding in my hands one of the first digital cameras. I played off his energy as well. I would say that I, the bumbling novice photographer, working the room as the brilliant professional looked on, would make a brilliant improv scene.

How I reacted to my own frustration would affect all those in that room with me. I kept my cool, and though embarrassed, I owned the em-barrassment-- I claimed it, making a statement to the world: "Okay world, I'm ready to receive with open arms and this is going to work out in some way." I claimed it and believed it. That's what improvisers do. My scene partners made it easy because they had my back.

Eventually I did find the buttons and got the shots. When it was all over, I had survived the session because I went with the energy in the room, grounded myself, and was truthful in my ability to play off others in the scene. My estimate-- about 70% attitude and 30% training. How do you train for the unknown anyhow? Study improv. Right?! There was also an unmeasured force of an unknown percent in that room. It was my scene partner's support that night. It was Joe Walsh, who by the way, has great comedic timing, and the Artist Relations Manager-- both having my back in that room. Support your scene partner.

Digital photography today is like tying your shoelaces. That night, bumbling actions framed the scene. It worked out well with Joe, and the Artist Relations Manager-- who took me to the shoot-- was too busy laughing to even think about getting mad. I am a comedian, but I wasn't trying to be one that day. I was just playing the scene with honesty, hoping I'd live to play another day. Joe Walsh was my scene partner. He made me look good. Thank you, Joe.

SELF SABOTAGE

Subconscious self-sabotage is a cancer. To avoid self-inflicted wounds, first open a dialogue with yourself such as, "What's up self, have some type of ego issue?" In improv we only have the present, so I urge you to step forward in the now. After all, it is improv. Everything you need you already have. Self-sabotage is like a self-inflicted gunshot wound. It hurts, it causes psychological damage, and it doesn't need to happen. It's especially pervasive in the arts. Since self-sabotage is self-inflicted and doesn't need to happen, why do so many performers engage in it, both on and off stage?

CAPTAIN KIRK

A friend of mine working on the bridge of the Enterprise buzzed my communicator with an invitation. She would beam me aboard if I accepted the mission to attend-- and I did. As the special assistant to Captain James T. Kirk-- er, uh, William Shatner in this reality, Shatner's assistant, responsible for organizing Shatner's day to day activities on and off set, was a friend. Shatner's wife at the time, Marci, who later drowned in a swimming pool accident, was appearing in a play in Hollywood. Therefore, I got an invite to the premier and I attended.

The Playhouse, located in the heart of Hollywood just north of Melrose Ave, was home to an exclusive group of thespians whose members included many A-list film actors. I was curious yet unsure of what to expect. The play itself was entertaining yet unmemorable.

Following the show's final curtain, the cast and invited guests shared cocktails in the foyer, to the side of stage. We all had drinks together while mingling. Just outside a picture window at the theater, I could see a contingent of Trekkies standing in the cold evening air, awaiting a glimpse of the Captain up close and in person. Perhaps there'd be a word from him as he left. Captain Kirk however is not the focus of our story.

I made my way through the crowd, sipping my cocktail, and chatting with guests. Mark Hamill of "Star Wars" fame passed me. He was in a foul mood. While focused on Hamill I nearly bumped into Jon Anderson, lead vocalist for the rock band Yes. We struck up a conversation.

As an improviser, I am sure of myself, but as a musician at the time I was having my good and bad days. I felt that performing professionally in bands was in my rear-view mirror. That made me unsure of myself as a guitarist. Yes, I was still a good musician, but my self-confidence was lacking. Being unsure-- that's when self-sabotage creeps in. It's the crack that self-sabotage looks for, giving you an excuse for not feeling like you deserve a particular prize.

BRIT ROCKERS-- **YES!**
Yes was a British rock group who, during their heyday in the mid-1970s, sold out arenas while promoting a series of successful album releases. They would eventually split up in 1981 and later reform in the 1990s for several more albums and a smattering of radio tracks. The reformed band would have changes in personnel. Yes had splintered at the time of our meeting and hadn't yet reformed. Members were playing with outside musicians. As a young teen, I'd seen them perform for capacity crowds at the Spectrum, Philadelphia's premier concert venue.

During my conversation with Jon Anderson, I revealed that I played guitar. This was on a Monday evening. After chatting with Jon for fifteen minutes or so, he invited me to a jam session that Wednesday. I was excited. He seemed to like me and wanted me to play guitar, to see what I could do and how I appeared on stage. Then came the drive home when I began to think about the invitation. Self-doubt began to seep in. I was a talented musician but knowing that Anderson's guitarist in Yes-- Steve Howe-- was a world class player, I began to second guess myself. Self-doubt was on the march and I was providing comfort.

Feeling nervous and in need of extra practice or maybe just subconsciously looking for ways to sabotage the offer, I set up a rigorous practice schedule exercising my fingers diligently and working on runs and scales. I made plans to attend the jam a week from Wednesday, not the Wednesday that was a day or two away. Not the Wednesday that I was invited to attend. I justified in my mind that I'd be giving myself a week of rehearsal - at least that was my thinking on the surface.

The following Wednesday, I arrived at the address that Jon Anderson had given me. It was a hotel ballroom. Unable to find any musicians, I approached the concierge perched outside the ballroom and explained, "I'm looking for Jon Anderson." There was a pause. "He's not here," the concierge shared. "Well he told me to meet him here," I said. "He's not here this week." "Oh?" The concierge went on to explain, "I'm sorry but last Wednesday was his last meeting here. He's left the country."

Uh oh, I was in shock. "What about the jam?" I asked sheepishly. He continued, "There is no jam this week." "No jam"…I mumbled to myself repeating the words of the concierge. I nearly dropped my guitar. "But Mr. Anderson personally invited me?!" I managed to choke out. "I'm sorry but the room is in use for a corporate function, Mr. Anderson has left the country." The words stung. I felt stupid.

In the swirl of preparation, it hadn't occurred to me that the day I was invited to jam might be my only opportunity to play with these musicians. Oh man. What drummer would have been in attendance? Probably a world class player. It had been a personal invitation and I had literally practiced myself into no opportunity at all. Had I not wondered if I'd be good enough, had I not doubted myself. Had I not psyched myself out...

Thoughts were swirling in my head. Oh, man. At the very least, I'd have had an interesting fun opportunity. As it was, I had nothing. I failed to believe in myself. I had fallen prey to the demons of self-sabotage. I didn't believe in myself enough to see that I already had all I needed. I already had the skills, and he seemed to like me. Passion and commitment and being in the moment would have carried me the extra distance. We often decide inside our head whether or not we're deserving, without even consciously thinking about it. We judge ourselves and pass sentence. For those who have experienced self-sabotage, you must know that somewhere down deep inside, you believed that you didn't deserve whatever opportunity had been presented. Self-sabotage is simply a lack of self-worth.

Creatives are especially susceptible to self-sabotage. How does the improviser overcome self-sabotage? How does anyone? Self-confidence and scene partner support help immensely. It's hard to feel that you know that you are all that you need right now, to accomplish anything. It's not always easy to know that you are the best *you* that you can be, and let your commitment and passion carry you through.

What if there's a chance you might fail? Failure is growth. It's okay. Boldly step into the spotlight and embrace the opportunity. You may fail, or you might just succeed. Either way, you are an improviser and improvisers face their fears. Improv prepares you to step forward and be counted.

When you hear the voice of the vulture that represents fear, when it sits on your shoulder and whispers in your ear, know that it's okay to be nervous and it's okay to acknowledge the fact that the vulture is sitting on your shoulder. What's not okay is for you to hand the vulture control. It has no power over you. Tell it so. Don't let opportunity pass you by. Don't sell yourself short. No regrets. You're an improviser!

CHALLENGE
Next time your improv group finishes a rehearsal or show, get everyone in a circle and then go around the circle and have each improviser give one positive comment to the improviser on their right, about something they did that night. Whether on an improv stage or in real life, we need to believe in each other more. We also need to believe in and love ourselves.

ATTITUDE

Improvisers with an attitude get the job done. Attitude is the complex combination of things we tend to call personality, beliefs, values, behaviors, and motivations. Attitude can fall anywhere along a continuum from very favorable to very unfavorable. Attitude translates to what we see when someone has an opinion. All people, irrespective of their status or intelligence, hold attitudes. All people have attitude. So I ask, how do you feel about your scene partner?

ROLLER DERBY

When other kids would arrive home from elementary school for a snack and to watch Captain Kangaroo or other kid faire that happened to be on television, I'd find the most arcane treats my dad had stashed in the closet or fridge-- from smelts to capers-- and then settle down in search of alternative after school television. It was always the same. I'd tune in the Bay Bombers female roller derby. They had attitude.

At a young age, I think I was about 8 years old; I knew all the rules and many of the players. Female roller derby was my sport of choice. My only sport of choice. There was just something about Roller Derby. Sure, the players were sexy, and I was a young lad, but it was the attitude of the players that kept my interest. It was their swagger after a bruising battle around the wooden track.

On the walk home from elementary school, I'd think of the tough sexy players. There was something about watching women who were so sure of themselves. Their moves were impressive, smooth, sexy and strong with a wild street edge. Of course, I was 8, but they made an indelible impression on my developing mind. I was bored in suburbia and wanted to be anywhere but suburbia. I could live vicariously through the actions of roller derby. And what was it I was really enthralled with? It was attitude. The teams had attitude and the individual players had attitude. I felt like I was a part of the action because of their attitude. Attitude staked their claim on my afterschool viewing time.

In improv, attitude can carry the scene. Though the first thing that pops into my brain when someone says attitude is a bunch of tough guys, but attitude isn't always tough. The dictionary tells us that attitude is a settled way of thinking or feeling about someone or something, typically one that is reflected in a person's behavior. Attitude is having a point of view or taking a stand. The improviser with attitude is more complicated and is interesting to watch.

Growing up, I lived for the excitement of living on the edge probably because I always lived in the burbs as a kid. My dad was often transferred for work and we'd move every three years, sometimes sooner. The only constant was that we'd always end up in the suburbs. When I graduated from college and moved away from home I headed west. I'd arrived in Los Angeles to pursue a career as a musician. It was on my way back from a jam session just after moving there, around 2 A.M., when I noticed a carload of gang bangers following me. I was aware enough to keep my cool. After noticing them, I made lots of turns to be certain they were in fact following me. They stayed with me. Suddenly I sped up, made a few more turns and then quickly slid into a parking spot where I ducked beneath the front dash clutching my guitar. I was just low enough not to be seen unless they stopped, got out and walked up to my car.

I heard their car slow as they neared my parking spot. My heart was racing. I hoped they weren't going to stop but wasn't sure. Seconds seemed like hours. Luckily, they didn't stop. After searching the general area, they eventually drove on. I'm sure they were hoping to catch me walking to my place, guitar in hand, where they'd hop out and take me down. I was scared. My heart kept beating heavily for quite some time. I thought it was going to jump out of my chest.

The carload of gang bangers had attitude. Lots of it. I had an altogether different attitude. I'd kept my cool and appeared calm on the outside but was shaking like a leaf inside.

Attitude, on the streets or on a stage, carries a lot of weight. In a casting session, the last thing a casting director wants is to see is a flat reading-- a reading with zero personality, zero attitude.

Roller Derby is long gone but memories of players boasting colorful names like Suzie Hotrod, Bonnie Thunders, Satan's Little Helper, Estrogen and Much Mayhem live on. What would your character's name be? In improv, give your characters attitude and use attitude to spice up your scenes. Roller Derby was about activity, competition, creating characters, teamwork, telegraphing information without words and moves. Doesn't that sound like a list of improv characters?

Think about the times in your life when attitude has taken an important role. Rewind simple events where the characters in your day-to-day activities had bold personalities, strong beliefs, values and/or motivations.

I was walking 6th Street in Austin, Texas on a Friday night. 6th Street in Austin is where all action happens on the weekends. It's filled with clubs and eateries. The street was packed with pedestrians that night. A couple of teenagers or maybe twenty somethings were hawking their talent for reading cards— tarot cards. They had attitude. I thought, "Okay, I'll bite." The girl seated nearby spoke. "Only $5!" I nodded. "Fine, let's play." Sure, I was game. I sat on some steps in an entryway to a business closed earlier in the evening. The girl threw three cards. It was evident she didn't know what she was doing. I looked her in the eye. "Ummm. I don't think so. You get a dollar for hustlin', but you couldn't read a signpost if there was one." I held those thoughts to myself, turned to the girl and with attitude spoke, "You can keep the five. Now let me read your cards!"

I had attitude and I shared it. The twenty somethings were confused. The scene had changed. Attitude gives your characters and your scenes spice. Give your improv characters a heavy dose of attitude, because scenes awash in attitude will hold the audience. People that have an opinion have attitude. Characters with an opinion are fun to watch.

THE TRUTH BEYOND THE TRUTH

Good improvisers find the funny in truth. Great improvisers not only find their funny in truth, but they also find the truth beyond the truth. There's no serum to get to the truth beyond the truth, just a willingness to go there. New improvisers often can't even be truthful. It takes time for improvisers to accept they can live in the truth of the scene and share honestly how their character feels. Many new improvisers don't yet understand that the funniest improv is based in truth.

THE TRUTH OF THE SCENE
There are two truths in improv - the truth of your everyday life and the truth of the scene. They can be one and the same but it's not necessarily so. The truth of the scene defines the scene. Improvisers should look for the comedy in the scene. Ask yourself what aspect of my character or this scene seems slightly off? Great improv scenes also often have a very unusual through line (which is the connecting theme that runs through the scene). This unusual through line might be based on an event or thing that is not accepted as real or okay in the world of your everyday life, but that can be still be accepted and justified in the world of the scene. Let me explain. If an unusual concept happens or reveals itself in the scene-- maybe it is something that couldn't or wouldn't actually happen in your everyday life-- you still can accept that unusual concept into the world of the scene as a truth. You accept the unusual thing by justifying it when you endow the scene with its usefulness in that world.

Truth, whether it's the truth of the scene or truth in our everyday lives, makes a strong foundation for the rest of the scene to be built upon. Often in improv, we want to play politely rather than deal in truths, truths that lay dormant just under the surface. What happens when those truths bubble up to the surface? First, when truth is revealed, the stakes become higher and the improvisers in the scene more vulnerable. Second, the scene's interesting quotient grows a thousand percent. Remember, the point of the scene is to engage the audience and hold their interest. Funny is an added bonus. Lasting funny comes from truth albeit from what angle the audience views that truth.

THE TRUTH BEYOND THE TRUTH

What is the truth beyond the truth? As adults, we share perceived truths, surface truths, and passable half-truths. They are all about acting politely. We politely scratch the surface conversation chatting about any subject that requires no depth. Characters in improv often suffer from these partial or surface truths. It's like partially committing to the scene. In your everyday life there is often partial commitment to friendships, jobs and relationships. What happens when you are all in? It's scary. However, your inner child wants to go there. It's okay. Allow it. Let's look at a couple of examples of the truth beyond the truth. To apply the concept, think how does your character really feel?

Today I received an email from iconic actor and political activist Martin Sheen. It was one of those letters where celebrities endorse a cause. Sheen, who is a long-time supporter of the UFW (United Farm Workers). The letter said he was concerned about the plight of the Farmers in today's political and economic climate. It was a form letter but seeing Sheen's name brought back memories.

I'd met Martin Sheen on the set of the television series, *The West Wing*. He stopped by just as the day's shooting was getting underway. Sheen was not in costume or make up and wasn't even due on set at that moment, but he just popped by to say hello to the cast and crew. Sheen did not differentiate between background and principal actors or above the line (suits) and below the line staff. He seemed genuinely interested in greeting everyone equally-- whether knight or pawn. That was his truth and he seemed well liked on set as well.

Fast forward five years or so into the future. I'd come to a Catholic Church in L.A.'s San Fernando Valley for my friend's daughter's confirmation ceremony. I'd never been to a confirmation and thought I'd show my support. It was a very long ceremony and my friend's wife, a fellow non-Catholic, talked me into taking a break with her sometime during the festivities. We walked out into the sunlight and sat at a picnic table on the church grounds, in a courtyard. I wasn't watching my surroundings, but then I heard a voice that sounded vaguely familiar. I slowly looked to my right. Martin Sheen was seated beside me at the corner of the same table. I hadn't noticed him before, when I sat down. He began talking to me. I really think he was talking to the universe while looking in my direction. In a tone of consternation, Sheen began speaking earnestly.

"You know how you can really love your kids and sometimes they just let you down. You know how you can love them and when they screw up you don't know what to do?" I nodded in agreement. "You raise them and do the best that you can." I was beginning to feel uncomfortable, mainly because he was speaking personal truths that felt too personal to share with a stranger. The sun beat down on us and it was a warm dry heat. I was suddenly aware of all that was around us. Sheen continued in a pleading voice. I believe at this point he was speaking with god. I just nodded once more in agreement. It was a moment of truth with the world stripped bare of all coverage, and I also felt naked and vulnerable, being witness and receptor to someone baring their soul.

I saw in those moments the truth beyond truth, and why Martin Sheen is such a great actor. It's in his eyes. Sheen's characters don't just read words, or speak words, they live them in the world of the stage.

As an improviser you don't have to take your truth to the level of Martin Sheen and bare your soul. However, as an improviser you should let your characters bleed. Allow them to feel and live in the moment. At the very least your characters should have an opinion about your scene partner, based in part on "knowing" how your character feels. How do they really feel? How do they feel about what was last said? How do you feel about what your scene partner has done or is doing? How does your character feel in general? Have an emotion fueled opinion.

Sometimes truth reveals itself without any words. I was working on the AM Los Angeles morning show, and film and television icon Carol O'Connor (*In the Heat of the Night, All in the Family*) was a guest. I'd gone up to the green room (where actors await being called to the set) to speak with one of the musical guests on the show. As I walked past O'Connor, our eyes locked. I knew that his son was a few years older than me and had some troubles with substance abuse and depression. Though Carol O'Connor hadn't said a word, his eyes spoke to me. I knew at that moment he was seeing his son in me. I stopped and softly said hello. He said hello back. We locked eyes for another few seconds as his eyes continued searching for something in me. I wished him the best and walked away.

In the above instance the truth was in the silence and spaces between our dialogues. When you're in an improv scene, try to have an opinion about your scene partner-- even if you are not sharing many words in the scene. You don't always need them. Feel what words are there even if unsaid. Feel your scene partner's character. Live in the moment of that character's personality. That is being truthful.

Truth in improv is not always heavy. Sometimes it's light. When I moved my mother into her independent senior living facility, I had lunch in the dining room with her. About half-way through lunch I noticed two substantially older women (substantially older than me) seated at a table across the room, waving at us. One had on a big floppy hat and sunglasses, like a character in a 1940's Grace Kelly film. I said, "Hey mom, I think they're waving at us." Then one of them started calling to us with, "Yoo-hoo! Yoo-hoo!" I looked over at them. The one with the floppy hat spoke. "Are you new?!" I answered, "No ma'am, my mother is the new resident."

CHALLENGE

Two improvisers face one another. One starts. They ask their scene partner, "How do you feel?" The scene partner answers by describing how they're feeling at that moment. There is no right or wrong answer. The second improviser does the same. One improviser may have said "melancholy" and the other might have said "radiant". That is followed by a scene with the two improvisers holding onto and using their beginning emotion. Live in the emotion as the scene plays out. About a minute and a half into the scene the improvisers should switch emotions. Continue the same scene but with each improviser living in the other's emotional state. Afterwards discuss how it felt.

OBJECT WORK

Object work is an important aspect of improv. Simply put, object work occurs when an improviser utilizes imaginary objects on stage. Great object work is achieved when an improviser is so proficient at object work that the audience believes they're actually seeing someone cook breakfast, read a book, play with a yo-yo or bait a hook and cast a fishing line into a lake. It takes talent to view the weight, size and multi-dimensional shape of an object in your mind, and then realistically share that with an audience.

Though not used all that often during performances, object work adds another dimension of believability to the scene. Object work also makes scenes more interesting to watch especially when done with commitment. Some scenes beg for object work so it's always great to have that extra tool on your tool belt.

"Click!" It was the sound of an imaginary camera at the hands of a school administrator. "Click," he just did it again. One more click was about all I could take. Here I was sitting in the Junior High Vice Principals' office, like a criminal awaiting trial. The Vice Principal, always the disciplinarian, was making what he thought was a point. I was trying to appear focused and attentively listening while at the same time tuning him out. I remember the words as he spoke them to me, slowly, "You do want to graduate Mr. Philippi, don't you?" After that all I heard was blah, blah, blah...

It was a B movie script ending with "…well then, it won't be in the cards, get the picture?!" It was at that point, the Vice Principal leaned in and I witnessed the object work, an excellent version of a large DSLR camera snapping my photo. (All I could think was, *excellent camera work!* I didn't know what improv was back then.) What a wanker. First, I was in Junior High-- not even High School, and second, I wasn't one of "those" kids. I was rarely in trouble. The Vice Principal thought he was giving me the scared straight life chat. What he gave me was my first memory of "object work", and it's still with me today.

Some improvisers are naturally good at object work, but anyone can perfect object work. I took a class, years back, taught by a guy who was just an okay improviser, but his object work was superb. He did this long kitchen scene where he was reliving the memory of his grandfather cooking breakfast. Man, I felt like I was right there in his kitchen with him and his grandfather. I could smell the hot food cooking. He knew where all the ingredients were, and when he turned over the eggs or flipped the pancakes-- it was real.

So, what's the trick to really good believable object work in improv? First of all, you have to feel the object in your hands. Let's say you're sweeping the floor. How does it feel to hold a broom? Okay, so you've never held a broom. Must be nice. Think of what someone on television looks like when they are holding a broom. When you make a call on a cell phone, hold the imaginary cell phone just like you would a real one. Give the objects weight, size, dimensions and texture.

Scenes that use object work are often more engaging than scenes with none. Object work can be used to create an entire environment like the improviser above preparing a meal in the kitchen while engaging his scene partner in conversation. We learn where the stove, fridge and cabinets are located, what ingredients they have in the kitchen, where the pots and pans are located and whether the stove is gas or electric. Cooking a meal not only creates an environment but gives both the audience and the scene partner details that add to the scene. Details might include how large the kitchen is and how experienced at cooking the improviser is, which tells the audience about the economic or marital status of the improviser, their age range, whether they are an urban or suburban dweller and more. These details also can be used in crafting the narrative as the scene develops.

KEEP IT SIMPLE
Sometimes the object work can be simple, such as reading a magazine or book in a waiting room, taking notes by hand, checking an imaginary wristwatch or the clock on the wall, bouncing a basketball

or my favorite-- playing with a yo-yo. Sometimes the simplest choice is the most powerful one. Besides, object work gives the improvisers on stage some business, something to do with their hands while the scene is developing.

When an improviser is bouncing a basketball, never make the scene about bouncing that basketball. Never make the scene about what the other improviser is doing—period-- unless you can tie that improviser's activity to your character. "Damn Jimmy, I've been looking for my ball all week and you had it!" "Didn't think you'd mind if I borrowed it." "Well I'm not running a rental store. I also want my baseball glove back this afternoon, as well and any other items you still have of mine!" The scene wasn't about bouncing the basketball or getting a baseball glove back but about the effect on the scene partner's life of borrowing the items without permission.

OBJECT WORK CAN INFLUENCE SCENE DIRECTION
Object work can also focus a scene in a particular direction if both improvisers are paying attention to the one another's work and supporting one another. The improviser who opens the jar of candy, then speaks, revealing the scene is taking place in a candy shop, or the improviser who takes a book from the shelf and makes a comment to reveal the scene is taking place in the research library at Harvard.

CHALLENGE
Use an object in real life. How does it feel? Remember the shape, weight, texture, positions of your fingers and hands etc. Now, without holding the actual object, use the imaginary version of the object and perform a task. Picture yourself using the broom, pen, phone, etc. as you showcase your object work. Sense the item's weight and shape. Try to be as realistic as possible.

Next pick a simple object like a set of keys. There can be many keys on a key ring or just a few. They can be modern small keys or larger keys, or even skeleton keys. Decide on what type of key ring the keys are on. Next use a key on the key ring to unlock something. Then use that same key again, but add nervousness to your action, then per-form the same task but add confidence, or anger. How does the emo-tion affect your use of the key? How does the type of key ring you've chosen affect your use of the key or the type of key itself? Try this same exercise with a paint brush, hammer or screwdriver. Add emo-tion to the action the second time around. Experiment with different emotions. How does it feel each time you change the emotion?

Lastly, this is an exercise for several improvisers. Start a scene with object work and let it affect the scene so that it takes the scene some-where. The guy with the fry pan turns the scene into the kitchen of an upscale restaurant where the staff is under pressure to deliver 5-star cuisine. Starting the scene with a hammer could turn into a cowboy stringing barbed wire during the range wars. Let the object work take the scene somewhere. Use object work at the beginning of the scene to create a narrative but be ready to change and adapt if the scene goes in a different direction.

Over a period of several days, observe and write down 3-5 items per day that humans use in everyday life, along with the activities that accompany usage of those items, i.e. brushing your hair, brushing your teeth, sweeping the floor. Recreate the activities on your list, in front of a mirror, or have a friend record you recreating those activities with their phone. Study the recording. What feels truthful? Remember to give the item realistic qualities and treat your mimed item as though you were using the actual physical item. See yourself going through the activity and commit.

PART TWO

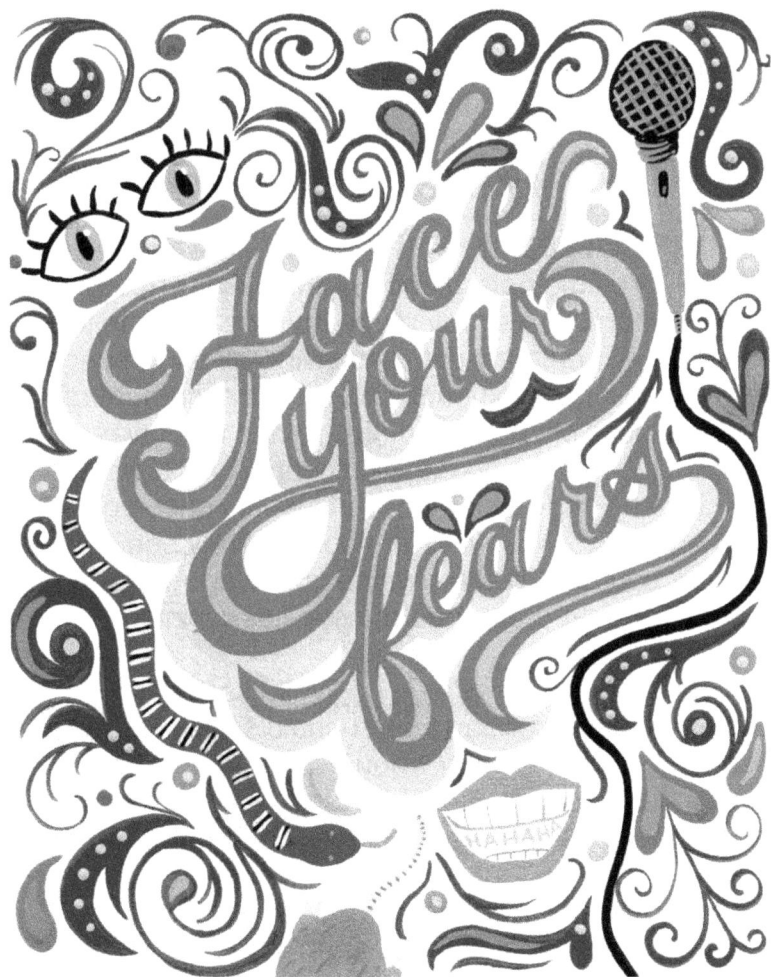

Face your fears

WARMING UP

In improv we warmup to shake the day off and get our minds and bodies in sync and ready to perform. Warming up also helps improvisers get in touch with their subconscious, sharpens reaction time, allows you a way to fine tune your creative engine, and get in touch with those around you as you tap into their creative energy. In street terms warming up gets the nimble meter ready to adapt and get nimble in a scene.

Scientifically speaking, warming up changes our brain function and frees up the creative part of the mind to operate at a greater capacity, while the analytic portion begins to scan for patterns and numbers, locking and unlocking doors and windows in search of connections.

TIME BEFORE COFFEE

Dateline B.C.-- the time before coffee-- the air was heavy with humidity. It was mid-morning; I slowly made my way from the parking lot to the restaurant. As I entered the restaurant, all things began to swirl and glow. My brain was experiencing a rearrangement of molecular density with no possible alignment. It seemed that I was caught in an endless loop, deep in the space time continuum. It wouldn't be until I'd had my first cup of Joe that the world would once again find some semblance of order. I was so tired I could barely see. At the restaurant reception counter, several waitresses were gathered around a sheet of printed paper. I propped my eye lids open.

How was I doing, the Hostess asked. "Well," I answered, "I'll be doing better once I have my coffee cause I could swear you were working on a crossword puzzle, though when I came through the front door, I found myself standing in front of that very paper, and I can now make out that it is clearly a restaurant seating chart not a crossword puzzle."

The Hostess seated me at a booth and I immediately began to daydream. A member of the restaurant's wait staff jolted me back to reality as she stood before me asking for my order. Still I was not yet warmed up. I'd had no coffee. This led to a second thought, as first thoughts often do, and that thought was that this restaurant's meals would be cooked to perfection. Why? Because the wait staff were warmed up. Still it was the time before coffee for me, and my hazy mind called out for stimulation. In improv, brain fog is not your friend- - I know this firsthand. Clarity of thought and the ability to focus both within and on your scene partner almost simultaneously are.

From an improv standpoint, the time before coffee is that time before class when every improviser needs to leave the outside world outside, sharpen their senses, bring them online and focus in. When improvisers arrive at rehearsal or class or a show, their minds are often still on the freeway or at the office or engrossed in conversation with their significant other. The warmup period clears the brain of stress and other thought that might impede an improviser from focusing in the now.

It wouldn't hurt people in their everyday lives to warmup before getting on with your day. That might include a positive mantra upon opening your eyes in the morning, and a piece of fruit or glass of water or juice as the first nourishment of the day.

If you've ever taken an acting class you've probably heard that your body is your instrument and it must be cared for which includes pre-audition prep. To perform as an improviser at your maximum strength, you must do the same, which is to warmup and fine tune your instrument. Improvisers deal in energy, and therefore must have all circuits warmed up and ready to function.

As a group in long form improv, we warmup to get all of our minds on the same page and we warmup for clarity of thought. Improvisers need maximum brain function for an improv show as well as to get the most out of an improv class. Improv warmups help us shake off the day and leave office pressures, household chores, relationship pressures and financial obligations behind. You can always wallow in that stuff later if you so choose. Improv warmups clear the mind and stimulate your thought processes and sharpen your reflexes.

When warming up it's imperative to get both the analytical and creative sides of the mind working in tandem. Word association exercises help. Giving and taking focus, sharing laughter, preparing to accept thoughts and emotions of others are all helpful. Remember improvisers deal in energy.

CHALLENGE
This exercise is for the improviser challenging themselves to warm up their mind without a scene partner or teammates. This exercise will benefit your improv performance by fine tuning your thought process and expanding your concept of truthful story telling while at the same time seeing more details.

This exercise is called *Pulling Back the Curtains*.

1) Select a location - any location that will allow you to easily have a clear view of a house, apartment building or a business (preferably during business hours). Your goal is to select any structure where people are within.

2) Seat yourself comfortably across the street or even down the block if you can clearly see the building from the outside. Your goal is to be outside a structure where people are inside. Your vantage point should be anywhere your actions won't be branded as creepy for staring at a building. Close your eyes and picture a black slate in your mind. Now open them and stare at building. Focus in on the rooms or area where you believe people are located.

3) Relax your stare and make it a gaze. Gaze at the wall to the room where someone is inside. A gaze is slightly out of focus and slightly off center. You're not looking directly at the spot where someone might be interacting with their environment behind the wall. Tell yourself you'd like to know more about the building and its inhabitants.

4) Picture the inhabitant or inhabitants doing things that people might do in a building of the type you're gazing at. Now tune them in. What

might they be saying? What exactly are they doing physically? If you've chosen an apartment building and it's evening and you're focused on one specific apartment you might see someone come home from a long day. They drop their briefcase in a chair, take off their coat and head to the fridge for a cold drink. You might see them preparing a meal or reading the paper on their phone or tablet in a favorite chair. Don't force anything.

5) Once you've created scenarios in multiple rooms of one or more buildings you've completed the challenge. Your brain should be warmed up at this point. The whole process might take 5-10 minutes max.

AM I WARMED UP?

Am I warmed up? You can smack yourself though personally I'm averse to inflicting pain or you can test yourself mentally. This is a trick I use from time to time; Make a list of average everyday occurrences like seeing an iguana on the lawn (I live in South Florida), making breakfast or sitting on the living room couch and watching television. Once you've noted a few ordinary occurrences flip the script on them.

Picture these daily occurrences in your mind in an unusual way. Maybe your couch is either no longer a couch or it does something unique and different. Seeing the world from new perspectives is an improv tool. So, what combinations might appear?

Perhaps iguanas guard my property and I pay them in vegetables, or my living room couch has been modified and is now a device I deposit cash into where it's magically deposited into my bank account. The couch could also be a transport device to alternate realities. Are you warmed up yet?

Our imagination is all that limits what we create. How we use those stage creations in the world of the scene is what separates a great scene from a weak one. The first step is to accept that there are two worlds-- the world of our everyday life and the world of the scene, and to open our eyes to the parallels between the two worlds.

I still haven't had enough coffee, but by this time I think all synapses are firing. My characters are starting to be well defined and my scene is grounded in a universe that makes sense. Ah, to be warmed up. However, my mind is stuck in a sparkly Sci-fi world, where I can transport my molecular structure across new frontiers, and all that seems clear is slightly off in some way. Okay, so maybe I need more warmup time or maybe I should realign my thought processes, ground my state of play and clarify my choices. Having confidence in yourself helps.

LIFE AS AN IMPROV SCENE
See life as an improv scene. Then look around. What can you identify in your everyday life that can transfer to the improv stage? How does your mind process the world? Have you ever asked yourself, "What am I really seeing here at the bank, the pharmacy, school, the office, etc.?"

Take a slice of your day, a portion of the day that's already passed, and think, how would my day unfold in an alternative universe if I focused on one unusual fact from my day thus far, blew that fact up and expanded on it. What would that world look like? Perhaps I had a large breakfast that day including nuts in my pancakes which might be unusual for me. In an alternative reality where nuts are magical how would that fact affect me? I'd put into motion the improv concept "if this were true then what else is true?" If I could put my mind in that space I'd be thinking, yep, I'm warmed up now. Let's get to work!

OPENING LINES

Every improv scene has an opening line. Though there is an exception to every rule, starting a scene with "Hello, it's nice to meet you," does not bode well for the scene's success. Yes, the scene must start somewhere. That's why you should start in the most logical place for an improv scene to start, IN THE MIDDLE! Improv scenes should always start in the middle of the action. Sure, your scene should have a before and an after, but starting in the middle of the action means the action and the story are already in play. Let's say you're going on holiday. Why have the scene focus on your buying the airline ticket and packing, when the meat of the scene is either something that happens during the flight or the action just after arriving at your final destination. Do yourself a favor, start in the middle of the action!

I like the challenge of trying different things and wondering whether it's going to work or whether I'm going to fall flat on my face. - Johnny Depp (Actor, Producer, Musician) Take chances! Dare to fail! You have all you need right in front of you for a successful scene. You are a successful improviser. Know it - claim it! Commit to making an emotional connection with your scene partner. Make the scene about them. Step out on stage and be brave. Start by making a short statement that demands an emotional response.

What about the opening line itself, the actual dialogue at the top of the scene? There are opening lines and there are opening lines. In other words, all opening lines are not the same. What you say at the beginning of the scene can be instrumental in setting the tone, connecting with your scene partner and/or introducing "game". Your opening line could set a positive tone putting the elements needed for a successful scene in motion or your opening line could cause a train wreck right out of the box.

If you start asking questions as you enter the scene, you are screwed! If you start conversing about someone not in the scene from the top of the scene, you're screwed! If you try to teach your scene partner something at the top of the scene, you are screwed! What should you say?

Opening lines serve two purposes. (1) They lay out the bones of the scene-- the who-what-where of the scene. (2) An opening line also should connect the scene partners emotionally. There are many ways this can be done. You can try being accusatory-- but if you do so angrily, and with too much vigor, you're screwed. If that happens, chances are that scene will start and end with an argument and you'll lose your audience. You can be nice, but nice is well-- it's nice, and that's not very exciting. There's nothing worse than being boring. How many audience members just dozed off?

On the other hand, your opening line can show your scene partner love. Make everything you say or do in the scene about believing in your scene partner's character. Let the opening line connect your character with theirs positively. Often "quirky" works well. Now we're getting somewhere. You could say whatever comes to you based on the scene suggestion or you could have a long list of possible opening lines that you select from.

WHAT MAKES A STRONG OPENING LINE?
What makes a good opening line? There are a few factors. A strong opening line is not too long and it's a line that helps your character find an opening to connect emotionally with your scene partner. So personal statements like "Drop and give me ten, Private!" tell the audience who the characters are to one another, where the characters are, and maybe even what the characters' statuses are, which can change during the scene.

A strong opening line can also merely establish a connection with your scene partner. "Bob, I'm glad you could get away to drive into the city for dinner. I've been wanting to speak with you about the Samson project." There is definitely emotion tied to this line and the audience wants to know why Bob was willing to drive into the city. There must be stakes. A line as simple as "Margaret, you make great coffee", also has merit as an opening line. We know the two characters know one another and we'll find out if they are friends or lovers or co-workers. We know the character speaking the opening line appreciates Margaret's coffee, and depending on how the line is delivered, may have other feelings for Margaret. We can then look at the scene from the standpoint of-- if that is true, then what else is true? Of course, the opening line could be a minute of silence that reflects the emotions you bring to the scene.

SLICE N' DICE DIALOGUE ON THE PBS LOT

"My boyfriend's gonna cut you! He's gonna cut you real bad!" Sounds like dialogue from the knife fight in *Rebel Without a Cause* or a line that would be at home in a *West Side Story* rumble. It is, however, a line of dialogue delivered to me by a women's correctional system inmate, on a television production lot. I was working as an Audience Coordinator on a talk show, shooting on the PBS lot in Hollywood. The show required a live audience, so they filled audience seats with tourists, softball teams, the occasional church group and busloads of inmates from various California women's correctional institutions. The show loved confrontational guests.

The institutions filling seats received a donation from the show, and individuals they bused in got to watch a TV show taping, and during a break, enjoy a slice of pizza and a soda. One piece. We always ran short so just one piece. This girl in line from one of the correctional facilities demanded two slices. I offered her the largest slice I could find but that wasn't acceptable. Then came those words above. What some people will do for an extra slice! I stepped out of reach in case she was carrying. Thing is, "My boyfriend's gonna cut you!" It's a line that demands, no it screams, for your scene partner to react emotionally!

JOHNNY DEPP IS ON THE PHONE

"Eww! Who's being Mr. Secretive?!" Johnny Depp demurred. It was another real-life opening line I'll never forget. I was the club rep for BAM, a California Music Magazine and had put a call into The Viper Room on Sunset Boulevard, a club Johnny Depp co-owned at the time. I was doing my due diligence to get some advertising dollars or at least an inside track on some great shows.

Anyhow, you know how sometimes you realize, after the fact, that you should do something, but you don't do it? Then, after the fact, you're like why didn't I do that? I couldn't believe I didn't engage Depp in conversation. Who knows, he might have even bought an ad. I could have used some improv training then.

After Depp said hello, all I could think was, "Holy sh**t, it's Johnny Depp. What do I say to him?" It's like having stage fright. Anyhow, like a nervous fool, I asked for the advertising guy or club manager who I knew wasn't in. Then Johnny asked who I was. I stuttered, "uh, me? I'm just a guy and I'm calling for so and so…" I felt dumb.

That's when Depp gave me his response-- "Ewwww! Who's bein' Mr. Secretive then?!" There was a pause. Then he says, "Well, okay Mr. Mysterious, is there any message?" I felt very tiny at this point but responded that I'd call back. Afterwards I thought--crap why didn't I talk to him? I kicked myself for a few minutes, then jumped in my car and drove over to the club across town.

Notice, I was second guessing my actions on the phone. It's the same thing improvisers do when they go home after class or following a show, and they replay their scenes over and over in their head. Of course, by the time I made it to the club, lots of time had passed, and Johnny Depp was long gone.

The line Depp said wasn't actually the first thing he said to me, that line was "hello," but you could open a scene with the line I shared. Given a choice, you should use that line. Compile a list of quirky opening lines that demand an emotional response and try them out in class.

SPECIFICITY

Specificity can make or break a scene. Dialogue without it can strangle the scene. Lines spoken in your scene such as "He had **stuff** to attend to" or "Dora needed help with **this or that**" or "Bob thought about **that** but never made a decision" should cause alarm bells to sound off. In the latter sentences, the audience is left wondering what "stuff" or what "this" or "that" might be referring to.

Utilizing specific details during a scene not only helps move the scene forward but is also helpful in defining characters that appear in that same scene. However, using specificity in your improv scene isn't as simple as spouting details. It's adding clear and concise language to point the scene in a direction. Using specificity shouldn't be the use of flowery prose either, unless that's a trait of your character.

What sounds better, "I bought a new car," or "I bought a 48' pick-up with flames on the hood, a 356 engine and a candy apple red metallic paint job"? The detailed ride with the paint job and flames on the hood, of course. However, you don't even have to be that specific. The scene calls for the type of ride you purchased because that helps define your character. Merely stating, "I bought a 48' pick-up" or "I bought a 48' pick-up with flames on the hood" gives your scene partner all the useful information about your character the scene calls for in order to move the scene forward.

THE NIGHT VISITOR
Specificity is improv gold. You can use specificity to set the mood and direction of the story as well as help define characters and clarify situations. Exploring the use of specificity in your everyday life can help you use it more effectively in your improv scenes, while sharpening your communication skills at home and at work.

It was the middle of the night when I first heard the footsteps on the wooden floor. As sleep cleared from my head, I discerned the pacing was that of a cat moving up and down in the hall. It was the pitter-patter of padded feet on our wide floorboards. The curious thing was that we didn't have a cat.

"All right who let the cat in last night? You both know I'm allergic…" were the words I shared with my flat mates. Of course, no one did any such thing. I was concerned. "Okay then, so how could a creature that large just appear?" No one seemed to have an answer. It wouldn't have been unheard of for my roommates to have played a trick on me. However, I was certain they would demand credit for their misdeeds and neither of them had done so. They were as dumbfounded as I. I chalked it up to just another average evening in a most unusual house.

The feline visitor appeared in my room several more evenings. I didn't know cats could be so damned loud I thought. Eventually I began to realize it was not only an unusual visitor but also other worldly. The visitations continued. First, I'd hear the cat out in the hall heading for my room. As I awoke, it would appear near my bed. Once I was awake it would turn and leave the room.

During our stay in the Craftsman style home, it became ground zero for many unusual experiences. Built in the early 1900's, the house featured hand-carved dark wood molding that ran throughout, with built-in leaded glass cabinets. We'd fallen in love with the place from the street with its heavy oak front door, oversized brass hardware and second story arched picture window. Our living room was so large it echoed as we walked across its turn of the century floor boards. Yes, it was a curious choice for three young 20 somethings to call home. When we moved in, the owner had said not to call him unless it was a matter of high importance, hinting that previous tenants having unusual experiences under its roof may have been bothering him.

Specific details up to this point in the story have painted a picture that sets the tone of the story while helping outline the who and the why of the scene. The audience yearns to hear pointed details that take the scene in a direction and help the characters along on their journey.

One night, the heat came on mysteriously and wouldn't shut off until the owner arrived to manually disengage it-- a day later. Needless to say, the heat was unbearable. Another time, my roommate-- whose usual routine was to unlock the door from the outside, come in and leave his keys in the lock facing the inside of the living room, so he could grab them quickly when exiting-- found his keys missing when he went to leave. Later we discovered his keys in the lock on *the outside* of the apartment as though he'd never used them to enter. The unusual events continued when a friend stopped-by, only to catch a glimpse of an apparition in our front picture window as she peered up from the street. Now there seemed to be a feline ghost moving about in the middle of the night and it favored my room.

Did I not provide enough kibble? Wait… cat spirits don't need kibble because they're not really appearing in my room-- or are they? If the kitty wasn't present in the physical, then why was I having an allergy?! It was a snapshot of a world most humans would find out of the ordinary and some would find scary. I continued to ignore the cat apparitions. Then again, it was hard to ignore cats from the great beyond. I just kept telling myself it was merely a slightly unusual dream-like state upon my waking-- but I knew otherwise.

The cat pacing culminated one night, when I awoke and looked up at my dresser to witness a large feline curled up on top. This cat was large, and it was white with beige markings. I sat up on the edge of the bed. Hmmm. How did you get up there? Next thing I knew, the cat was on the floor, and when it had my attention, it headed for the bedroom door. It turned as if to ask me to follow. So, I did.

My new friend then turned down the hallway where I'd heard the sound of other cats that had been pacing on previous nights. I followed my feline friend out into the long dark hallway, where the cat and the sound of its footsteps disappeared from view and out of ear shot, as it was swallowed by darkness. I went back to bed.

I wasn't sleeping well. A few weeks later, the phantom cat returned, and its footsteps could once again be heard in the hall, outside my bedroom. They were just loud enough to wake me. One morning around 4 a.m., my clock radio turned itself on. I thought it was time to get ready for work and began to stumble out of bed, before I realized what the actual time was. A song came on my clock radio, and the vocals sang "Get," which was repeated several times, and then the channel moved to another channel that was playing a different tune. A singer was finishing with the word "Out!"

I turned off the clock radio which I never used and had not set. Was it all in my head or was I experiencing a metaphysical incident in the physical? The hair stood up on the back of my neck, but I was tired and managed to go back to sleep. Twenty somethings can do that…

The next day I called a friend who was familiar with such mischief. Valuing her opinion as both a friend and an advisor who deals with such phenomenon, I sought advice. She suggested I should move. A week later I was in a new place.

A few days after I moved out, my female roommate had a guy over who fell asleep with a cigarette, and though it was our policy not to let anyone smoke in our place, the cigarette caught her mattress on fire. Luckily the alarm went off and everyone got out. The Fire Marshall's report concluded that our place was just minutes away from going up in an impressive blaze. I gave thanks for the mysterious cat who led to my moving.

IDENTIFYING SPECIFICITY

The dictionary defines specificity as the quality of belonging or relating uniquely to a particular subject. With that in mind, let's go back over the cat visitation story above and identify places where specificity is effective in moving the scene forward.

Here are some examples:
(1) "All right who let the cat in last night? You both know I'm allergic." This line of dialogue explains an action and shares a glimpse of character dynamics and how my roommates and I might interact with one another. We also learn that I'm allergic to cats plus the fact that a cat has visited. All provide specificity and are pivotal pieces of information key to the scene's direction.

(2) "The cat pacing culminated when I awoke from being asleep and looked up at my dresser to witness a large feline curled up on top." This piece of specific information tells the audience that what's happening is important and definitely a haunting and not something silly.

(3) "One morning around 4 a.m., my clock radio turned itself on. I thought it was time to get ready for work and began to stumble out of bed, before I realized what the actual time was. A song came on my clock radio, and the vocals sang 'Get,' which was repeated several times, and then the channel moved to another channel that was playing a different tune. A singer was finishing with the word 'Out!'" The specificity of what has just happened says that the scene must make a turn as the scene reaches its pinnacle.

Now it's your turn. Take another look at the story above and identify a few other spots where specificity adds to the story, helps define characters or gives events clarity or purpose. Apply the same ideas to an event in your life. Write it down and identify the specificity.

SHOW DON'T TELL
Specificity provides great ammunition for creating visual landscapes and in improv, it is prudent that you show, not tell, whenever possible. Take for example someone arriving home. As you put the key in the

front door, if you have to go through a keyring filled with keys to find the correct key, that would tell the audience and your scene partner something about your character, and possibly about the place you're entering. If you use a long heavy skeleton key as opposed to a modern key, that will tell the audience something different than if you punch numbers into a keypad rather than using a physical key. As your character opens the door, if you convey its weight and height-- that can tell the audience something else about the type of place you're entering as well.

Let the details you reveal show aspects of your characters' status, habits, likes and dislikes and when possible, show, don't tell. When you give details, think of them as giving the scene ammunition. You will later be able to refer back to those details as needed, to enhance your scene, your character, and your interaction with your scene partner.

CHALLENGE
This exercise utilizes specificity as a tool to strengthen your improv scene work. Pick five places you might consider visiting such as a national park, a museum and the library, etc. Make a short statement about each of the five places on your list, one at a time. For example: "The National Park is a peaceful place," "The museum is large," and "I do my research in the business section of the library." Each statement should say something about each location. Next, add specificity to each statement you've just made.

Ask yourself why is the National Park a peaceful place? Think, what statement best describes how large the museum is? You can use different words but keep the meaning and add specific details. For example, regarding the park you might say, "As I'm seated on this bench looking skyward, I can finally paint that landscape." Regarding the museum you might say, "The museum is so large you can land a plane in it." For the library you might say, "I was in the business section of the library working on my research when I got the call about a promotion at work."

If you do this exercise with a scene partner it's your scene partner's job to build on the specificity you've laid out, or vice versa, with a line that moves the narrative forward and keeps the focus on your relationship. For example if you said "The museum is so large you can land a plane in it," your scene partner might respond with, "Yes, it would be a great place to have the company party if they're willing to close museum for a day. You always do go big!" You can use specificity to further define characters, the relationship between characters, or why these characters are in a particular location as well.

FACE YOUR FEARS

Every improviser will eventually have to face their fears. My fears may be different from yours, but both are just as real and both are as crippling to the scene. Once you begin to face your fears on the improv stage, the stronger your improv play will be for doing so. Plus, the more you face your fears head on, the quicker they will dissipate. If there's a subject you don't like dealing with or a type of character you're uncomfortable playing or playing opposite, at some point you are going to come face to face with that subject or character in your scene work. **You might as well get it over with now.**

When I'm in a fearful situation in a scene on stage, I don't pretend that the fear doesn't exist-- I look straight at it and acknowledge its existence and while doing so acknowledge that this fear I'm experiencing has no power over me. Don't pretend like you have no fear. Embrace the fear.

Improvisers have both unconscious and conscious fears. Conscious fears are the easiest to face because you know you're walking into the fire to face this type of fear. Unconscious fears hide in the darkness and attempt to manipulate from the shadows. Once the improviser is aware of the unconscious fear it can be faced head on and banished. Both stand in the way of great improv. Both exist in our everyday lives as well and stand in the way of your success. Tell unconscious fear to step out of the shadows into the light. Tell both types you know they exist and to shut up because you have a job to do. Focus on something you want to accomplish rather than on the fear. How do you face your fears in everyday life?

FEAR IN THE OPERATING ROOM
As the nurse's aide ran his key card through the scanner, the large door with the ominous 'no admittance' sign opened to the pre-op area. I was shown to a prep cubicle with a bed. Heart palpitations came in waves, causing me to flash back on early improv perfor-

mances, when I was scared, and waiting in the wings, before an improv show. It was the same feeling. Fear of the unknown, and of what could go wrong, swept over me.

Fear is real-- yet it isn't. Fear manifests in the physical, yet fear is manufactured mentally. In improv, the fear in your mind is created by you, as a protection mechanism-- yet it protects nothing. In improv, my telling you to face your fear is easy for me to say but I've been there myself. When I first started to improvise, I was deathly afraid of the stage and performing. I've come a long way and so will you. Note that in improv, fear dissipates the more we step up and come out to play.

As an improviser you can refocus fear or negative energy and overcome those fears, once you are aware that you are being fearful of a situation. Fear refocused manifests as a stronger performance. Nerves can become your determination to succeed.

Fear is all in your head. I'm not saying it isn't real because it sure as heck feels real if you are experiencing it. What I am saying though is that fear once acknowledged can be controlled and used as a strength, rather than as a weakness. However, that day in the hospital, there was no stage, so nothing to do but shake it off or at least attempt to. Sometimes in improv, shaking it off is the key-- telling fear it has no power over you. Fear, I know you're on my shoulder, but you have no power over me!

My scene was playing out in real time. "What makes this day more important?" I thought. I was about to go under the knife for an operation. Fear began to creep in once more when one of the two nurses assigned to me focused her attention on finding a suitable vein to connect my IV drip. A second nurse informed me that they'd need to shave my tummy and groin. Ah yes, scene partners-- working in tandem for a common goal, hopefully not to shave your groin but yes supporting one another. Scene partners should be working together to get the job done, smoothly and efficiently. Always have your scene partner's back. I hoped that was the motto of the nursing staff at the hospital.

My mind was racing, and the fear started to creep back in. What if something goes wrong?! I'll be asleep I told myself. Oh okay. Then I told myself, to check out the nurses. Like good scene partners they were doing an awesome job working together. Remember, when your scene partner looks good, you look good. It works out best for all involved.

Both nurses left my bedside cubicle, pulling curtains across the doorway. I could hear their conversation on the other side. Who would shave me? The improv equivalent of being a scene that is stalled at its pinnacle, with neither scene partner ready to make a move. Really? I thought. They're arguing about who should shave me? Give me the damn clippers. Second thought, better not.

Turns out the official shaving committee was backlogged, so the soft spoken, kind, early 20s nurse began the process. Whew. Close one. Half-way through, she was called outside and replaced by a tall hulking man with 3-4 days growth of beard, an island accent and no smile. Damn. This was the life equivalent to an improv scene where everything suddenly comes to a halt. A scene where clarity is gone.

In improv terms, it was an unexpected change of scene direction. It was the entrance of a new character that held the power to change the balance of the scene. In improv, we must be prepared for anything. Easier said than done. I'd have to grit my teeth and force a smile knowing this man knew his craft and I'd be okay.

Following my shave, I requested a bathroom break before surgery. A nurse had to follow me closely holding up my IV, forcing me to take tiny steps like a 90-year-old man in bright yellow hospital socks and a flowing green gown. I got into character, as I made my way to the toilet. The sight of me resulted in chuckles from patients, nurses and loved ones in adjacent pre-op bed cubicles. I wished someone had filmed that. I knew they were laughing because I was scoffing at adversity, and laughter works wonders.

I'd relieved a little tension, and at least I wouldn't pee on the surgeon. Back to my tiny silly steps. I am certain that absurd looking would have been an understatement to describe me. The improv translation of my situation was truthful character work, layered and quirky. Probably I just looked dumb. Finally, the surgeon came in to re-assure me, all would be checked out before the Anesthesiologist sent me off to dream of new adventures.

In improv, there can be a scene which has a few false starts, and maybe falters, until someone really adept at the craft, steps in to save the scene. Everyone in the scene knows this improviser is the ultimate scene partner. They really listen and their creative juices flow like Niagara Falls. At that point the weaker improviser can be emboldened, and the scene has a happy ending. Of course, it's better when both scene partners carry their weight…

Remember, improv mirrors real life or does real life mirror improv?! Look for and make note of characters, scenarios and emotional connections in your day and hopefully we will not cross paths in the Operating Room!

PLAYING AGAINST CHARACTER

Playing against character type in improv often gives a scene the ironic twist it needs to reel in an audience. Playing against character type guarantees an *unexpected* twist. Some examples of playing against character type might be the Astronaut that hates flying, or the bunk house Cowboy who lives to create "cake" masterpieces with his artistic baking hands.

In improv, playing against character says you are expected to behave in one way within the context of the scene, but for some reason, your character behaves in an unexpected way in the context of the scene. Playing against character type can also be you, playing an established archetype, but opposite what an audience might expect of that archetypical character. A great example I saw once was a two-person scene that featured a police sergeant who was a former ballet dancer assigned to the front desk at the police station. The scene juxtaposed the gritty work of a detective with unintentional ballet moves he'd brought into the scene from his former career. It was a hilarious scene. The characters in the scene each had a former career that affected their current career in some way, like a movement or way of speaking, but it was never out of context with the activity directly addressed, which made the scene even more hilarious.

ADAM & THE ANTS MEET BLACK SABBATH

Adam & the Ants were a new English rock act with a single that was climbing the charts. Adam lit a special fire under his west coast U.S. fan base with the help of radio station KROQ in Pasadena, California, whose program director chose to mirror the English charts.

At that time, my buddy and I were in an original alt-rock band together. He was living with his girlfriend who designed stage clothing for touring rock acts. Metal masters, Black Sabbath, were one of her clients.

Sabbath had an upcoming tour and were due to be fitted for stage clothing. As the sun's glow in the west illuminated the skyline one last time, before turning to darkness, the faint whisper of music could be heard on the sidewalk, moving toward my buddy's apartment. Black Sabbath bassist, Geezer Butler, and Sabbath drummer Bill Ward, boom box in hand, were walking together, enjoying a light-hearted sing-along with a tune blaring from the boom box.

Adam and The Ants latest release, "Antmusic", was the tune that could be heard bouncing off the pavement, as musical notes exploded from the speakers with the Sabbath rhythm section's voices singing along, as they closed in on my buddy's ground floor apartment.

Improvisers often play against character type. When an improviser is expected to play a specific type of character because that's the type of character he or she usually creates, or because the improviser has a specific look or voice tonal quality and the audience expects a specific type of character but the improviser chooses to play the opposite, they are playing against character. Playing against character type in improv keeps the audience engaged. An example might be me playing a gangsta' rap character or larger than life urban pimp. Neither are characters one might expect to come from me. Playing an archetype such as a jewelry thief but one who steals jewelry to polish it and put it back is also playing against character. Playing against character can be very effective because it shows a new character perspective or turns a story on its head.

BLACK SABBATH SING-ALONG
Black Sabbath was one of the heavier bands on the charts when their first few albums were released and thought to be purveyors of the dark arts, their music conjuring images of witches, spells and magic and projecting evil upon the land. Adam and The Ants, on the other hand, were known for quirky alternative rock. Adam and his band were part of the new wave movement-- two opposite schools of thought interwoven for a moment. As an improv scene, the dynamic could translate to improv gold.

Members of Sabbath were having a sing-along to an Adam Ant tune. What form of sorcery is this? That is the question Black Sabbath fans would be asking had they been privy to the events of that night. What form of sorcery? What form of sorcery indeed?!

Black Sabbath and Adam and The Ants were two points of view at a point of intersection. In improv terms, scenes are brilliant when opposite points of view intersect and give the audience an ironic situation, a skewed point of view, an unexpected point of view. In the above instance, it was as though one side was playing against character type. It was not only unexpected, but it was also a gift.

Playing against character type can heighten the emotional game of the scene because it highlights unusual behavior that becomes a game, once a pattern is established. We see Sabbath bassist, Geezer Butler, humming along with a new wave tune, rather than checking out some other heavy music. His doing so is an action of greater significance at that time than it would be today. The serious, brooding, heavy band enjoying a moment of silly playfulness.

As improvisers, we have the opportunity to play against character type whenever we want. Actors, not so much. Actors are often seen by casting directors as fitting in a particular category, or particular few categories. For example, they may say actor "X" is right for a role as lawyer, detective, CEO and Chief of Police, and actor "Y" is a great fit for the role of suburban dad, salesman and/or construction worker.

Casting directors probably wouldn't send a guy they feel is right for suburban dad roles, to audition for a serial killer. Actors can be type cast when they play a specific type of role for a long period, and then casting directors and network execs only see them as playing that type of role. Improvisers don't have those limitations, though they may have several go-to characters. Improvisers can choose any type of character they can think of and make it their own.

DOES IMPROV HAVE TO BE FUNNY?

Seriously man, does improv have to be funny?! The juxtaposition of the sentence before this is funny. Okay, well it could be funny. However, the answer, unequivocally, is NO! What? I thought improv was supposed to make people laugh. Sure, we all, for the most part, relish that moment when the room erupts in laughter. However, improv is really not about being funny. Improv is about being interesting.

Ever think about making the audience lean in and listen to your expression of a tender moment, or perhaps make them gasp during an intense moment, or break their hearts? It happens from time to time. Sometimes scenes are just a slice of life and that's good too. The scene may have serious moments, even if the scene just touches on the serious like an episode of "Seinfeld". Once the funny comes back-- and it eventually will-- the funny bits will get even more laughs. Having the audience engrossed in your serious improvisational skill is an art in and of itself.

New improvisers try to play their scenes like an out-of- body experience, in other words they are not present in their own scenes let alone emotionally invested. New improvisers think they have to reach far and wide to find something to latch on to, when everything they need for a great scene is right in front of them. Your scene doesn't always have to be funny either-- just make it interesting. Remember, improv is everyday life that has a little extra something going on-- like adding icing to a cake.

I don't like sports. Now don't get me wrong, I do like to exercise, and as a kid, was a runner on the track and cross-country teams in high school. I even won a few medals. So, when I was invited to play softball by an entertainment industry Artist Manager, I hesitated. When he explained there would be all comedians on my team, and coaxed me by bolstering my ego, I thought-- why not.

I also know practically nothing about sports, so he had to play to my ego as if saying, you got this Greg! Yeah, maybe I can hold my own watching a Lakers game after having the rules explained because I'm a quick study, but I'd still confuse an anthill with a pitcher's mound if I'm in the game. They do look the same you know. I actually stood on one barefoot-- an ant hill that is. One thing I am certain of, is that fire ants' equal pain, but that's another tale.

THE TEAM

Back to pumping up my ego. "Come on Greg, it's only softball...you should play! It'll be fun. Besides, the teams will all be made up of comedians!" I wasn't a comedian. I was a music guy, but I thought-- what could go wrong? Excited to play, I went out and purchased a glove and a pair of cleats. It felt official, I was now a softball pro.

Truth is, I'd never played softball, but I figured the sport uses an over-sized extra-large baseball. Gotta' be able to catch and hit that. I'm in. Then, that first Saturday, I overslept and missed the game. Oops!

The following week, I was ready to go. The game took place on a baseball field across from the Universal Studios backlot. Our star player, SNL alumnus Kevin Nealon, was on the pitcher's mound. Unfortunately, I overslept again, arriving in time for the last couple minutes of that second game. I didn't play. At least I got out of the house and into my car.

I was determined to make the third game, so the following week, I set two alarms, woke up on time, and hustled out to the field early. I was one of the first to arrive. However, there was a fence around the field, and this particular Saturday, the gate was locked. Tough break. Then someone said, "let's just jump the fence." No big deal. Game on! To show my gung-ho commitment, I was one of the first two guys over the fence. When I landed on the other side, I struggled to get back up off the ground. "Uh-oh. Not sure it should be this hard," I thought. Eventually I was able to finally get up and head to the outfield.

I played the entire game in the outfield. I deserved to be relegated to the outfield. I suck at softball, plus I missed the first few games. Luckily no one got a hit. After the adrenaline rush of the game wore off, I knew something wasn't right. I'm glad we hadn't chosen log rolling. Checking in with my body I found there was an issue. I couldn't stand without assistance and definitely couldn't walk without help. Intense pain set in, which sent me to the doctor.

The doctor prescribed pain killers, wrapped my knee, and put me on crutches for a month. My softball career had just come to an abrupt halt. The next day, I was on a plane headed to Nashville for work. It was a long painful flight. In Nashville I struggled to get from one location to another in excruciating relentless pain.

My hate-hate relationship with team sports had actually started years earlier. In high school, for example, we were supposed to be wrestling in gym class, which I hated with a passion-- not gym class, just wrestling. I thought wrestling was just for the guys in the silly costumes on television. I got a buddy to wrestle with me and told him we'd just choreograph the whole thing and put on a show. I guess my choreography was lacking.

The coach caught on and made us really wrestle. I got an elbow in the eye, which led to a black eye. It was a real shiner. It made me look tough. This allowed me to play a role and impressed a girl from a visiting high school band who would give a concert at our school that evening. After the concert I got a dance out of it with the girl, and she got James Dean, well, a reasonable facsimile—me! All thanks to my black eye.

THE YING & YANG OF THE SCENE

As an improv scene, the above story has both moments of happiness and moments of tragedy. Not tragedy in the sense of a death, but there's a 'ying' and 'yang' that pulls the scene from one emotional direction to the other. For example, an improviser could play the above scene in an uplifting manner with tender moments, or tug at the audience's heart strings by playing the misunderstood anti-hero baring his or her tortured soul. Yes, the scene may have humorous moments and they should be played for maximum effect but playing to the scene's other emotional moments makes a greater impact on the audience, than just playing for maximum laughs from start to finish. Improv does not always have to be funny. It does have to be interesting. Audiences demand the scene be interesting.

I was once in an improv scene about two brothers that ran a mortuary and we played the scene seriously, focused on the relationship between the twisted brothers. The audience was riveted to their chairs. The scene became funny about 4 minutes in. That was when the crowd erupted in laughter. Four minutes by the way, can seem like a lifetime up on stage. It's those moments *between* the funny that are just as important if not more so, to building a solid foundation for the characters to operate within. Most improvisers just want to be funny, they strive for funny, but those moments between the funny, when played truthfully and with passion, are just as important as the moments that garner laughter.

CHALLENGE
Outline seven true stories that have taken place in your everyday life during the week. That's one true story for each day of the week. You may think, "I don't have seven stories." The thing is, you do. These stories don't have to be life changing. You went to the grocery store, or the gym, right? You definitely went to work. Think about events that happen as you go about your daily routine.

Write a few paragraphs about each story, nothing complicated, just outline what happened and describe a couple of characters. Keep the stories in a notebook. At the end of the week, look over the seven stories, and for each story, make a list of approaches from which you could attempt to tell the story on an improv stage. An approach could be from the female heroine's point of view as a loner, or if writing about a visit to the grocery store, add that it's the day the circus came to town so maybe your point of view is with curiosity. If you're writing about that visit to the grocery store, your approach could be with frustration or anger or jealousy.

Describe each angle or approach in a sentence or two max. Keep in mind that strong emotions and/or looking at the subject matter from a skewed viewpoint will be the most interesting approaches. Don't try to be funny.

Bring your list to an improv group, and in pairs of twos, improvise versions of the stories, exploring the different angles and approaches. Have both improvisers enter the scene from the same point of view or approach, then let the scene go in whatever direction it chooses to go in. Once you've tried a few of these short pieces, change an element in the scene such as adding an unusual location, or state that everyone in town is a former Olympic champion, etc. Discuss what worked and what did not.

WHO - WHAT- WHERE

Defining the WHO-WHAT-WHERE of the scene is the important skeletal structure for an improv scene, that if brought out in the first few sentences, gives the scene everything it needs to flourish.

WHO-WHAT-WHERE are three important words that provide points of intersection and a solid foundation for the two improvisers on stage, as they start a scene. Providing the who-what-where, is setting the skeletal foundation that will allow an emotional connection between the characters and pave the way for elements of game, while engaging the audience. Introducing the WHO-WHAT-WHERE, at the top of the scene gives your scene the basic elements needed for your story to stand on.

TEQUILA MEXICO / THE CARTEL HWY

I had traveled to Guadalajara, Mexico, a city of one and half million, located below Mexico City and inland from Puerto Vallarta, along a corridor of highway dotted with desert scrub and agave plants, on either side of the highway for miles. One morning I hired a driver to take my wife and I to Tequila, Mexico-- birthplace of the drink that shares its name-- about 40 miles outside the city.

I inquired with the driver about his favorite Tequila, which was a boutique brand that until then, I'd never heard of. Being adventurous, we agreed to visit his choice for a tour of their facilities, which was located somewhere outside the city of Tequila. I now had the WHAT for the scene.

Leaving Guadalajara, we took the scenic route, passing a field artillery battlement with uniformed army regulars in fatigues and helmets, bearing automatic weapons. They also had a Howitzer at the ready, in a sandbagged enclosure. Had I missed something on the news? Perhaps an uprising or cartel insurgents?

WHAT

The "what?" What is happening in the scene? Not what are the improvisers doing, but how are the improvisers affected by the action in the scene, and what is going on between the scene partners? How do the scene partners relate to one another based on what is happening? Remember, that the scene is about the two characters themselves, and how they feel about one another-- not the action itself in the scene. If a teen is bouncing a basketball, how does his buddy feel about him bouncing the ball? Is his buddy upset he never gets a turn, or happy they have control of the ball because it's a tournament and now they might win?

With Guadalajara a speck in our rear-view mirror, we arrived at a crossroads where a lone, dilapidated, wooden fruit stand stood, its silhouette casting a long shadow on the desert scrub. Our driver pulled off the highway, and a guard in a tattered and dirty uniform emerged from behind the fruit stand. Looking out the window, I noticed there was nothing for miles in any direction. Now the scene has a WHO. There are many options for the "who," from our driver/guide to virtually anyone we encountered that day.

WHO

The Who asks one question-- Who is in the scene? It's a question that either scene partner can define for themselves. The scene partners can also name one another. The WHO can be anyone. Often the simplest choices are the best. They are usually the most honest.

I wound down my window, and the guard shoved his pump shotgun through the opening, pointing it at my chest, while yelling at the driver in Spanish, demanding our passports in an unfriendly tone. My wife who was with me, is thinking we're gonna die. Me, being an eternal optimist, or maybe just naïve, is thinking all will be fine. Turns out, the guard was just attempting to exert his authority. At least that's what I chalk up his edgy trigger finger to, as we sat in the car just outside the chain link gate by the dilapidated fruit stand. We now had the WHERE or at least one possible where.

The smell of gun grease and sweat went up my nostrils as the guard's torn shirt sleeve dangled near my face in the hot desert air. The guard was screaming at our driver, demanding we hand over our passports. Our driver was calm. He's got this. The guard eventually put down the pump action shotgun and opened the locked chain link gate, with its barbed wire accoutrements. We were allowed to pass. One hurdle down. I'd just broken a sweat.

Soon we were bobbing up and down over rough unpaved terrain, which continued for another mile or so along a dirt road. I could see we were headed to a clearing with several structures. A cloud of dust was following not far behind. We stopped at the clearing, in front of an ancient farmhouse in need of paint, and by a barn and several smaller farm buildings. Far from any signs of civilization, a tinge of fear began to creep in-- but only a tinge. This was an unusual Tequila manufacturing operation.

WHERE

Clearly establish where the scene is taking place. The location of the scene, THE WHERE, can be useful in the relationship between the improvisers on stage. If you have several possibilities be specific about exactly which where you are establishing, so the audience and your scene partner are certain as well.

Either scene partner can define the specific location where the scene is taking place. If the scene is taking place in a house, think what room are the improvisers in? If the improvisers are in the kitchen, for example, then what type of kitchen is it? Is it a turn of the century Victorian, or Craftsman house with an over-sized range and leaded built in cabinets, or a small kitchen in a bachelor apartment with a hotplate? Details give your scenes an extra dimension. Regarding the WHERE, location details help define who your character is and how your character lives. Keep that in mind.

The audience for example might be aware the scene is taking place in the kitchen, because one of the scene partners is making break-fast. The details in his or her object work define the type of kitchen.

Always show, rather than tell, in improv. It's a visual medium. The improviser making breakfast can use certain appliances, or move about in the space in a particular way to give the audience and the scene partner a feel for the type of kitchen-- i.e. size, status, etc.

There are many interesting locales and people to be plucked from our daily lives that we can bring to life and explore onstage. Too often we forget to establish a who-what-where, or we forget that our lives are fertile ground for harvesting experiences from.

Back at the Tequila farm, someone with authority has located a young woman who can speak English. We enlist her for a tour of the grounds. One of the most interesting parts of the very short tour was the small shack where they cook the blue agave plants that make tequila, in a giant vat that appears to be a hole in the ground. The liquid is heated at high temperatures, thus killing any disease, which, while I was in attendance, included many insects who'd parked them-selves on the surface of the hot liquid. We also visited the barn which was a maze of tubing like a giant lab experiment.

After the short tour, I walked across the complex, to a farmhouse in search of a bathroom. Two men dressed in all black-- from their fitted leather jackets to their black slacks, shoes, dark glasses and slicked back hair-- are inside, and motion for me to sit with them for steak and eggs. Though they don't look like they're in the Tequila business, I'm hungry. Just as I'm about to sit, I catch my wife out of the corner of my eye, using hand signs to urge against the move-- so I decline the offer.

Up to this point in an improv scene, I'd have many locations to choose from, and I could do so in any number of ways. The WHERE could be anywhere-- from the shack where the alcohol is heated and si-phoned off to the barn, the farm house, the grounds outside any one of the buildings, and the fruit stand where the guard stood. The WHO could be any one of many people I'd come in contact with that day, and in improv, I might choose to build a character from bits of characters I'd met. The WHAT could be my search for quality tequila taking precedence over safety, or the driver's need to take us places that regular tourists don't go, which turn out to have danger attached.

Remember that the WHO-WHAT-WHERE are introduced at the top of the scene and help to establish a direction for the scene within the first few lines of the scene.

THREE SIMPLE WORDS
If you can define three simple words-- WHO-WHAT-WHERE, as they happen over and over in your daily life, you can easily name and identify the who-what-where of your scene. A simple concept, with three simple words. It's a matter of getting in the habit of naturally identifying them in the first few lines of the scene. Once you do the scene will have a solid foundation for you to build on.

U BENT HEIR!

You are here. Where are you?! U bent heir-- that's Danish for you are here. It's plastered all over the Metro in Denmark-- that particular saying. It's a reference point. It could be anywhere, and so could you. The Danish Metro is a wonder. It's so clean you could eat off the floor. Not that I'd recommend it. Of course, you have to dodge an army of bicyclists to get to the Metro station first, but that's part of the charm. U bent heir. Well I know I'm somewhere. If you focus, you might just have the clarity needed to identify your location. Concentrate.

However, if you haven't named a specific place as being *here*, how can you actually know where here is? Ah, but you are an improviser, therefore you are a detective. You're on a subway car. Why would someone want to eat off the floor of a subway car? That, ladies and gentlemen, is what the improv scene is here to explore-- but you'd better explore the topic seriously if you want the audience in your corner.

Oooh! Ahhh! It's a scene, and there are lots of ooohs and ahhhhs. It's as if the audience is glued to a death-defying high wire act, and you're in the center ring, high above them. The trick is to be focused.

FOCUS
Just like any one of you reading this, I don't always know where here is, because I'm not always focused. I know I'm somewhere. In an improv scene, I get to define where that somewhere is, and label it as "here". Here could be here in your sister's closet, or here in chemistry class. I don't remember my high school even offering chemistry class. I do remember biology. I always had a conflict when they were dissecting something. I'd get excused to go run around the track. The team needs me! Back to chemistry class. If we did have chemistry class, it would have been like "uh-oh, Johnny's burning something in class again." That's why the teacher sets him up in the far corner of the classroom. Now that would make an interesting improv scene. All the above would make interesting scenes, and they began with the concept of "you are here." U bent heir. I'm feeling very Danish today.

Not sure how feeling Danish can be explained, but the concept is interesting.

Improv games need your focus. Take the improv game Five Things. An improviser has to announce five detailed somethings, connected to the topic given by another improviser. The five things the improviser calls upon, from his or her subconscious, bubble to the surface, while at the same time, that same improviser's conscious mind-- which is now under pressure to produce-- is looking for ways to add humor, specificity and/or mystery, while announcing the Five Things.

"Give me five stories from your childhood." That's no fun. Not very specific either. How about, "Give me five horror films about a burgeoning minnow population that has never revealed themselves, because they were just too gruesome for human consumption!" Cool, but maybe there are just a few too many details, and your answer is in one long run-on sentence. A more specific statement might read, "Give me five horror films dealing with the gruesome effects of minnow death syndrome."

Speaking of not identifying where you are-- I've been there. I don't always know where here is myself. Once I was unfocused, and my being unfocused was almost the end of my life.

We'll start here: The car door was open and there was a gun in my chest. Seated in the driver seat, I knew it was a life or death, do or die moment, the type of moment that defines you. I wanted to shut the car door and rewind my life for a do-over. No rewind for this guy. My gut told me to make him, the guy with the well-oiled 9mm, the perp, see me as a person-- not a thing. I looked away. He swore and demanded my wallet. I dared not correct his use of expletives. I spoke calmly. "Hey man, do you mind if I keep my license, you know what a hassle it is to go through the DMV to get it replaced." I pleaded. It worked. I'm here. Now I know where I am.

Today you are here wherever here is. There is no promise of tomorrow, and the past is the past, so how are you going to grow your improv game? First, take one afternoon and allow that afternoon to be your time for improv growth. I was working it last week.

WHAT'S REALLY GOING ON?

Last week I was in Home Goods, and a woman pushed past me with her cart. "Excuse me!" she mumbled with intensity. Those were her words, but the tone of her voice said, "I'm in a bad mood, so get the fuck out of the way!"

That same day, I was in the lumber department in Home Depot and a guy stopped to ask if I was almost done. "How many more (meaning pieces of plywood) do you have to have cut?" Those were the words. What the actual tone of his voice and look on his face said was, "You're taking forever. I should take precedence because I only have one piece even though you were here first. I also am doing a repair job I don't want to be doing, so hurry the hell up!" Grumpy!

At The Habit, a sort of healthier fast food spot, the girl at the register ran the order before allowing me to add a drink on it. She was being efficient, and I was being indecisive. I had been pondering and moving slow. My wife looked at her and said we'd pay separately for the extra drink. She didn't look at my wife but at me, and said, "Oh hey, don't worry about it." Those were the words. Her body language and voice tone said, "you were very nice, and you ordered something healthy that I personally recommended and also enjoy, so I'm going to comp the drink," which she did.

Often, we don't pay any attention to those around us as we go about our business. If we take a moment and pay attention to the details around us, the world might just reveal itself as outstanding in some way. Sure, things could go south, but the positive thing-- if that happens-- is that it's warm there. At that point, you'd know where you were. We know improv is a conversation or interaction with another that is made up on the spot. You should know that. You are an improviser. What you may not know is that one of the reasons a bad improv scene is bad is because the improvisers in the scene are not talking about each other and/or how they really feel, nor are they introducing truths. They are talking past one another and are merely parroting what they think others expect them to say, or they're trying to be clever, or they think they can outsmart the scene so they're saying words they think they can get away with hiding behind. BAD, BAD, BAD! That's not what I'm really thinking but you'll never know. The scene knows. You're not reacting honestly. You've been outed.

Some of the greatest character work in improv is an improviser speaking as themselves and letting the character define how they move and what is of concern to them. It's not just doing a funny voice and figuring you've got it covered. There are times for a funny voice, but isn't it more interesting to watch a surgeon who's addicted to daytime television miss his last patient in a do or die situation because he was caught up in a daytime drama on the little screen? Not only did the surgeon miss the surgery, but he didn't care because the soap was so good. Now that's an addict and it doesn't require a funny voice or silly walk. Remember where it all started? Yep. The red dot on that Metro map. U bent heir. Now you know where here is because it's wherever you define here to be.

GET OUT OF YOUR HEAD

How many times have you been in an improv class and the instructor yells out, "Get out of your head!" I had this instructor at Second City and those words echoed across our classroom often. Those words meant get out of your head and get back in the scene.

An improviser is on stage and the scene stops for a brief few seconds. The improviser is in his or her head rather than in the moment, trying to write the scene rather than discover the scene, trying to control it. The improviser on stage is about to find out the scene cannot be controlled like that.

You think you have to be in control because grown-ups are taught to control the conversation and/or control the process whenever possible. However, SURPRISE, you are not in control! This is improv so hey man, let go! When you are in your head and not in the moment, you might as well not be in the scene, because for all intents and purposes, you are in fact not in the scene. If that's the case, the scene will NOT reveal itself to you.

WHY ARE YOU IN YOUR HEAD?
Sometimes improvisers are in their head because they've established a bad habit of stepping out of the moment due to fear, which takes them back into their head. It sucks to know that fear is giving the orders. Other times you're in your head because ego has taken hold and ego says you must be in control. Then there are the times you're in your head because the improviser is being a grown-up and grown-ups are taught not to let go. Whatever the reason, you must get out of your head and get back in the scene.

THE VISITOR
My roommates and I were living in an early 20s craftsman style home in the Hancock Park section of Los Angeles, which had been divided into a fourplex. The oversized oak trees, other apartment buildings,

and craftsman homes on our street stood as remnants of another era, dark and mysterious.

Our second-floor abode boasted an oversized picture window in the shape of a large half-moon with a view of our tree lined street. We put a couch not too far from the window so we could look out on the city. The interior of the apartment, with its dark wood, built in leaded glass cabinets and carved beveled crown molding, was an ornate throwback to early 20th century opulence and mystery. The large half-moon picture window let in enough light to offset the dark wood in our mystery cave.

A friend stopped by to visit after work one evening. Wind rustled through the trees as she hurried up the sidewalk toward our door. While doing so she noticed a woman in our picture window enjoying a cocktail. Damn it, they're having another after-work cocktail hour and they didn't invite me! Though our friend didn't recognize the woman she waved anyway, continuing to our door figuring the party was in full swing.

TRYING TO CONTROL THE NARRATIVE

If this had been an improv scene and the girl running up the walk, our friend, was in her head trying to control the narrative she would have forced some action into the narrative, whether it was a natural place for the story to go or not. In a scene she might say something like, "I couldn't get in the door, so I climbed in a window. They certainly will not get away without inviting me!" She would force the story in a particular direction before it had even unfolded.

An improviser who is in their head attempting to manipulate the scene may not seem so bad on paper, but on-stage opportunities to connect characters, explore emotions and concepts are often lost when one of the improvisers on stage is in their head. If the scene were allowed to continue and be discovered, we'd see twists and turns and the unexpected might happen as it does in life.

That day, our friend rang the bell and knocked. No one answered. She backed up to the street so she could get a better view. The figure in the window was still enjoying her cocktail. Our friend began to get frustrated. She waved again but still there was no response. Our friend then ran up to our door where she pounded loudly-- at least as loud as her small aspiring writer fists would allow-- all to no avail. At this point she was thinking we had the music turned up, only she didn't hear any music leaking out onto the street. Funny thing, there was no music. None at all. Disappointed that we weren't responding, she eventually left. The woman with the cocktail watched her leave.

That night our friend found out that neither me nor either of my room-mates had been home. The apparition she saw in our window remains a mystery to this day. There had been other mysterious visitations. Eventually that event, coupled with other strange occurrences, like the ongoing feline spirit visitations in my room, convinced me to move out shortly thereafter.

Life often has twists and turns. When we allow an improv scene to unfold and play out as life, it will have twist and turns. Get out of your head, and let the scene unfold.

CHALLENGE
This is an exercise to keep improvisers in the moment and help them stay out of their heads. It's designed for two improvisers. The improvisers get a suggestion of an object. The first improviser builds a character using the suggestion in some way. Then that character delivers a monologue-- sharing details about who they are, what they do, and most importantly, how they feel about themselves, others around them, and life itself. Emotional investment is important. When improvisers are emotionally connected, listening and focused on one another, they are not in their head.

When the first improviser is finished with his or her monologue they should freeze. The second improviser then repeats the process. Once the second character finishes doing their short-detailed monologue, the two characters do a scene together, looking for ways to emotionally connect within the scene. When the scene begins, the improvisers must justify why they're in either one of the two monologue locations, or in a third as of yet named location.

Doing the above exercise helps keep the actors out of their heads, especially if they focus on creating a character and then focus on connecting with their scene partner emotionally. Focusing on your scene partner's words will help keep you out of your head and focusing on making a scene partner look good in the scene, is helpful as well.

RHYTHM OF THE SCENE

Everything in life has its own rhythm. On the stage, improv scenes each have a rhythm. Thoughts also have a rhythm. Everything in life has its own rhythm. When you create a character tied to the rhythm of the scene, you can navigate the scene's intricacies much easier and connect with your scene partner and with the audience, on a deeper emotional level.

BURT LANCASTER
Burt WHO?! Burt Lancaster is an Academy Award winning actor, named the 25th greatest actor of all time by Cinema Archives, and the 19th best male actor of all time by the American Film Institute.

Occasionally, I'd go running during my lunch hour, when I worked in the Century City office complex on the west side of Los Angeles. At times, I'd end up on the Beverly Hills High School track, just down the street from my office. Academy award winning actor Burt Lancaster also would jog on that very same Beverly Hills High School track. One afternoon, it was him and me, and a slight breeze…

Burt Lancaster, dressed in a gray track suit and wearing an English driving cap with a towel tucked around his collar bone, seemed to be talking to himself. I thought it was odd. The man was getting up in years. I ran past him, and upon closer inspection, it was evident that Lancaster was learning film dialogue.

I was watching the process of an Academy Award winning actor, a film icon, at work on his craft. Those moments were burned into my brain. Lancaster was reciting his lines while circling the track, and at the same time, he was shadow boxing. He was doing so at a slow steady pace. The ebb and flow of the rhythm in his work was evident. I'd been taught that great actors use the rhythm of the scene to give their performance weight, just as improvisers use the rhythm of the scene for heightening the scene they're in.

Burt Lancaster was working the rhythm of the scene in real time. He understood the connection between his character's overall persona and how the pace of his dialogue and his character's emotional state, coupled with the cinematographer's shots, fit like pieces of puzzle in creating the Director's vision. Improvisers can thread a live stage version of that same needle.

THE ANALYTICAL MIND MEETS THE CREATIVE

It's important for improvisers to be able to use several different parts of the brain at the same time while still working in sync with the rhythm of the scene. There are improv exercises that assist with this. In layman's terms, it is like walking and chewing gum at the same time, or mental multi-tasking. An improviser who is in the midst of a scene and present, and working in the moment with their scene partner, while at the same time digesting a suggestion and/or listening for gifts or looking for patterns that can be turned into game play, is using mental multi-tasking. If the improviser is also locked into the rhythm of the scene, their job becomes much easier in focusing the creative and analytic, while moving the scene forward.

As an improviser, how can feeling the rhythm of the scene show its importance? The answer is that when you are feeling the rhythm of the scene and you connect with that rhythm; you'll have a greater connection between your character and what is happening in the scene. In music you can either count the rhythm by reading notes and rests or you can feel the rhythm and roll with that.

To know the rhythm of the scene in improv is to feel it. Listen with your body and feel the scene in your gut. When you purposefully reach for and attempt to step into the rhythm of the scene, it will meet you with open arms. What does your gut say? Be intuitive and trust your feelings. As Burt Lancaster shadow boxed while reciting his lines, he was working with rhythm to cement those lines in his memory. Feel the rhythm-- it's all around you. As in life, so it is with improv.

In film, it's the rhythm of an edit, or the pacing of shots. On the stage, it's the actors' dialogue delivery that propels the scene-- moving the story forward. In improv, it's just you and your scene partner in a room feeding off one another. Feel your scene partner, feel the scene and look for patterns that you can use to move the scene forward. There should be a gentle push-pull, a back and forth that will build and eventually reach it's pinnacle. Allow the rhythm of the scene to speak to your body. Use the periods of silence, relish them, let them work for you.

CHALLENGE
This is an easy exercise to warm-up a group of improvisers while giving the group a feel for connecting with the rhythm of the scene. The exercise is Doot-do-do! Get a group of improvisers in a circle and set a tempo by having everyone snap their fingers or lightly clap their hands in unison. Start slow and later you can pick up the pace when the group, as a whole, is comfortable doing so. Throughout the exercise the clapping or snapping in rhythm continues without stopping.

The first improviser in the circle yells out a word. Example: "shoe" and the improviser to their right in the circle, yells out another word perhaps "lace" in this case then the entire group yells out the two words together. In this case, "Shoelace! Doot-do-do!" This is done in conjunction with the rhythm of the group's finger snapping or hand clapping. Then the next improviser yells out another word perhaps "hat" and right away the next improviser to their right yells out another word perhaps "rack" then the entire group yells out the two words together—"hat rack, Doot-do-do!" Yelling out your words and delivering them within the established rhythm of the scene is much more important than what words are said. Run through the exercise a couple of times then stop and take a look around. Notice that as the group gets more comfortable with the exercise, they start to speed up the process. The object of this warm-up is to keep the group feeling the rhythm of the scene and delivering words within that rhythm, whether the rhythm is slowed down or sped up.

LET THE SCENE BREATHE

I often harp on letting the scene breathe. It's because improvisers are often in such a hurry to get wherever it is that we're going, that they forget to slow down and taste the scene that is unfolding so vibrantly before them. We often do the same thing in our everyday lives. To let the scene, breathe is to give it air, to put space between the dialogue, and know as an improviser, you don't need to fill every second with words. Check in with your surroundings and your physicality, use object work or just pause and take a breath.

The following event has been slogging about in my brain for nearly 30 years, like a muddy boot print on a newly tiled kitchen floor. It left an impression. The night I told the following tale in public was at a Story Slam in South Florida. That was also the night I realized that science doesn't have all the answers. The reason I chose this story as an example of letting the scene breathe is because there's nothing like a ghost story or tale of the absurd to bring out the breathy bits in the story genre. I assure you; this tale did happen as I describe it and though these events may sound strange, and to some, unbelievable, I'm telling this tale to the best of my recollection truthfully.

BLACKER THAN THE BLACK OF NIGHT
I awoke in the middle of the night at a girlfriend's apartment. Stumbling out of bed I stood up slowly to make my way to the bathroom. The apartment was pitch black except for a nightlight in the bathroom, which was located on the other side of her large dining area outside the bedroom. Standing, I felt my way along the bedroom wall in the darkness moving toward the doorway that led into the dining room, letting my eyes adjust to the dark as I slowly made my way.

Entering the dining area, my eyes first rested on the large rectangular dining room table with seating for eight that filled the space. Scanning the dining area as I moved into it, I noticed something in the corner of the room. It moved-- which caught my attention. I stopped. It was leaning forward while grasping the back of a dining room chair. I stood stunned, frozen in place for a few moments. This thing in the room with me was blacker than the black of night, humanoid in shape, and slender. Its head on top was in the shape of a conquistador's helmet, with a sort of pointed ridge. I took a step forward, then stopped. What was only a matter of seconds in hindsight, felt like hours. We stared at one another.

MOMENTS OF SILENCE

In improv, those seconds without any dialogue leave an opening for object work or space work, or to check in with your physicality. Improvisers don't have to always be speaking. Silence and silent space in scenes are welcome. Silence allows the scene to breathe. Silence also gives improvisers a chance to interact with their environment. Most improvisers feel they have to fill every moment with chatter. I'm here to say you do not! Relish the power of silence. Use the silence. Take your time. Let the scene flow. Don't force it.

In both slow play and fast play, scenes should breathe. In slow play scenes, letting them breathe is natural spacing. On the other hand, what to watch for in slow play scenes is letting the scene breathe to the point where the scene stalls. This doesn't happen often but can. In fast play improv, there is still a need to let the scene breathe. The pace of fast play improv is unique to fast play improv, but once again, scenes don't have to be wall to wall dialogue.

Back in the room, as I stared at the slender humanoid, its large slanted eyes were bright red and glowing, and it was looking back into my eyes. The hair on my arms stood up as did the hair on the back of my neck. Suddenly the creature was seated in one of the kitchen chairs with its legs crossed. I was frozen with fear yet fascinated. This creature I was observing, didn't walk to the chair, it just was standing one minute, then appeared to be seated before me in the next few minutes. Then it did something unusual. It smiled at me. This was highly unusual because visually the creature had no mouth. At the same time, I knew it was smiling because we were communicating telepathically. The creature was sending images to me.

There is no dialogue in the above passage of the story. In an improv scene, that would be time to explore the space. Show the audience whenever possible-- don't tell them. Object work could come into play at this point in my story. Object work adds color to a scene by utilizing objects that aren't in the physical but that are realistically portrayed in the scene, such as adjusting a picture on the wall, or pulling a small flashlight from a night stand, or looking out a window. All of these engage the audience. An improviser can use object work to add details to the scene while painting a visual picture of the location.

When improvisers do object work, they often use sense memory to recall the feel of an item such as the feel of an apple, or of a soft ball in your hand-- to help portray holding it in the scene. In improv, it's important to give imaginary objects size, shape and weight, as though the item is in the physical.

The creature was no longer seated and now appeared to be standing on the far side of the table with its arms folded, and still it was staring. Once again, it hadn't walked around the table, it just appeared in a new location around the table. I was now focused on one thought. I've got to pee. Sure, I was scared, but I figured if this creature was going to hurt me it would have done so already. I figured I'd come up with a question by the time I came out of the bathroom; there were many formulating in my brain. Minds work oddly, late at night, when the bladder is a consideration. If I'd only known not to drink all that water or coffee or whatever liquid I drank earlier that evening. If I'd only slept at home that evening. If I only didn't overthink what I'm writing now.

When I came out of the bathroom the creature was gone. I held this story for years. Then one evening at a psychic reading, I was told I could ask one question. As I opened my mouth to ask the question my guide spoke. "Was it blacker than the black of night?" I replied "Yes." "Did it have glowing red eyes?" I replied "Yes!" It was then explained to me in a way that didn't make much sense. That night, I gathered I wasn't supposed to know the whole truth. After the reading, I only shared my story with a few people, then I put it to bed for years. The question remained-- what had I interacted with? Ghost? Alien? Demon?

Years later I was doing research online and using the various search engines on the web to look for information. My mind flashed back on that night, so I typed in my description: i.e. blacker than the black of night, along with the creature's shape, and the fact that it had glowing red eyes. A story came up someone had written, about seeing the same or a similar creature in their apartment. Unfortunately, they were not as calm as I was. They ran out of the apartment screaming. I tried to reach out, to write them through the internet, but their story was old, and I received no answer. I still wonder about that night, now with renewed questions.

All improv scenes tell a story. Baring the tale itself, and the unusual nature of my particular tale, can you see how scenes can speed up and slow down, but have the most effect when they take a breath? When you are in an improv scene remember to use the space and know that you don't always have to speak. Sometimes to show and not tell using no dialogue whatsoever is the most poignant use of your improv talents.

MYSTERIES AND SECRETS

Great scenes are filled with characters and scenes shrouded in mysteries and secrets. When the concept of mysteries and secrets comes into play, the audience can taste the intrigue, but not quite put their finger on it. Mysteries and secrets are not tangible things in acting or improv. The audience gets a whiff of an unknown spice which keeps them guessing--a taste you can't quite identify. Mysteries and secrets often live in a sly smile, a raised eyebrow, or a mild reference to something of intrigue. I was first introduced to the concept of mysteries and secrets by an acting coach decreeing its importance to dramatic acting and multi-layered characters. I soon found that mysteries and secrets can be successfully applied to improv scenes and improv characters as well.

THE PARISIAN

Calling her name was like ordering a French croissant, but was she really French? It really didn't matter. She seemed so. Her essence was pure Parisian and mysterious. My cubicle on the executive floor of a large entertainment conglomerate was adjoined to that of Binette an attractive, soft spoken, alluring young French girl. Binette had petite features, long hair and European fashion sense. Her eyes spoke with an innocence that seemed to call out to older successful men like a beacon from on high.

I was a young administrative assistant in my twenties by day and a starving musician by night. I was also one of only two men out of thirty-five or so administrative assistants on the executive floor. Life was simple then, and Binette, the girl in the cubicle beside mine, was my pal.

Great scenes are often simple scenes, filled with characters that have unexplored layers of mystery living in those scenes. All great drama has mysteries and secrets and in today's world so does some comedy. Great characters have mysteries and secrets only discernible by the clues in their eyes and movement. A place can hold mysteries and secrets as well. The concept of mysteries and secrets makes a character alluring and hard to pin down, yet able to draw in those close by.

An attorney in our corporate legal department, whom we'll call Bob, often took Binette to lunch. I never officially met Bob, but I did catch a glimpse of him twice. He was a well-dressed, well-groomed, well-financed older guy (probably only 5 years or so older but in those days, it seemed like decades). Bob was much farther up the corporate ladder, and into Binette.

Bob, man of mystery and his well-polished shoes, would whisk Binette off to five-star eateries and private clubs for an extended lunch, while I dined at my desk in my cubicle, or on special occasions, enjoyed a sandwich in the courtyard below.

On the days when I was certain Binette would be dining in a Beverly Hills eatery, I would be sure to wait at my cubicle for her return. Even the napkins cuddling her warm leftovers, smelled of luxurious surroundings and occasionally gave my nose a taste of her perfume. I savored her leftovers and she knew of my appreciation. It became a ritual.

The story above, at this point, paints a picture of a character driven story, where the mysteries and secrets of the characters themselves, linger in their dialogue and actions. Surrounding the characters and narrative are mysteries and secrets which the audience is exposed to. It piques their interest.

One afternoon Bob had taken Binette to an upscale steakhouse. Binette, the petite young woman who ate like a bird, ordered a large NY steak. When the check came, Binette asked the waiter to box half the steak. As the leftovers were being boxed, Bob turned to her and said, "Did I just buy lunch for Greg?" There was a long pause. "Maybe I should just take him to lunch next time." Though the offer was facetious I would have accepted...Bob knew how to roll. Binette left the entertainment industry and Los Angeles to pursue a career in fashion. I knew little of her new endeavor except that mystery and secrets surrounded her and her new position.

My instincts about Binette's fashion sense were spot on. When I asked her how she got the job-- moving from an administrative assistant position in television to something creative in fashion design-- speaking in a soft voice, she cracked an innocent, albeit sly, smile. In a sweet, somewhat laid-back manner, she said it was merely a matter of having confidence and je ne sais quoi. I was impressed. To this day, I believe it was her mysterious Parisian persona, and she knew it.

When Binette moved, I adopted her houseplants, and felt honored I'd been asked to do so. As I picked them up from her west side apartment, I could feel her mother's eyes upon me and I could picture her saying, "So this is the guy who eats your leftovers." After that we lost contact, and it was good we didn't stay in touch. The plants she willed to me died soon after her departure. Who knew that house plants could provide such a challenge to keep alive? My days of gourmet dining were also behind me for a time.

The plants had died but Binette's aura of mystery made an impression. Just as great film characters live in an aura of mysteries and secrets, in improv when we play the scene in truth, utilizing specific details, the mysteries and secrets of the scene come out to play. Trust your gut. Let your instincts guide your state of play. The mysteries and secrets will weave their way through the scene. The audience may or may not laugh, but they will be engaged in the action, and find the scene interesting.

Characters should be multidimensional. We are complicated beings and as such, our characters should also be complicated. In improv characters often have simple wants, but below the surface, so much more should be present. It is up to us as improvisers to explore those areas. Long form improv allots the space in which to do so. The resulting scenes may not be funny but must be interesting.

NEW IMPROVISERS

New improvisers often step into a scene and touch only the surface of the scene. This is due in part to newer improvisers being afraid to delve deeper into building their characters, or because they forget that the scene is about establishing emotional connections between those characters. Some improvisers have trouble connecting on stage because they are wrapped up in what's going on in the scene, and they talk about what's going on rather than about each other, which is a mistake. Other improvisers are in a hurry to get a laugh, which shouldn't be a priority. There is a difference between going for the joke and laughs that come from the truth of the scene. The latter takes more skill.

As you make the emotional connection with your scene partner-- get personal. Reveal bits of who you are and who you are to one another, but not everything. The exchange between the two characters in the scene should have rich layers of emotions and of appreciation, attraction, deceit, sharing, and so on.

Our improv characters, much like the characters we create in life, should reveal many shades of emotion. The mysteries and secrets of the character lay hidden just below the surface, and on occasion, bubble up to the surface and into the scene. This is just as true on stage as it is in your everyday life. Responding to a scene partner's line with a double entendre or short answer that gives information but leaves more to be revealed keeps the allure and the audience stays on the edge of their seat. Mysteries and secrets of the scene. A valuable tool.

CONFIDENCE MYTH

An improviser I know recently auditioned for Saturday Night Live. It was the second or third time. The audition was a call back. Call backs are always a good sign. That means the powers that be liked what they saw and want to see more. Lorne Michaels, creator of SNL, flew to Chicago to watch the improviser on stage. Kudos to the improviser for even securing such a prestigious audition!

It was 4 a.m. and I couldn't sleep so I got up and began writing. After an hour or so on the computer, I decided to give my mind a break and peruse social media. Bam! There it was-- in cursive writing, on the Facebook page of the improviser who'd auditioned for SNL-- "Mindset is everything". I had set out early that morning to write about the confidence myth, and those words-- "Mindset is everything"-- were the perfect tie-in. My point could not be made more succinctly. Mindset is everything. So profound. Bam! It hit me again. Mindset truly *is* everything.

First, I have to ask, is confidence a myth? Could be. You are at an audition and there are three improvisers on the back wall. The first is the shaky improviser trying to focus his or her nerves. At the opposite end of the spectrum is the second improviser who just doesn't care about their performance at all, probably because they are not committed, therefore they're not nervous. Their performance will lack spice. The third improviser is the egotistical improviser. This improviser sucks the oxygen out of the room and is tough to play with because they are not playing to make their scene partners look good. What type of improviser is going to be cast? There is only one type of improviser who will always get the job done. That's the improviser with the right mindset.

Every improviser and every type of improviser brings a unique energy to the stage-- but what about their confidence? Let's say you're about to give an important presentation, and you clearly know the subject. That might involve confidence, but that same presentation might also involve ego. There is a fine line between confidence and ego. Does an improviser have to have confidence to give a solid performance? The answer is no. What do you need in order to have the right mindset, to give a solid performance? You need to know your craft and be well rehearsed.

Often your improv confidence onstage is a facade that you project, while actually cowering inside and that's okay. The more the improviser has trained in the craft, and is prepared, the more that improviser can appear confident. Just as in any business situation, it's all about having the right mindset for the project at hand.

The goal is to appear on that stage or appear before the executive team without ego, on an even keel-- to not speak or act too effusively or too lackluster. That same concept applies to both you as an improviser in the world of the scene and to the world of your everyday life. Be prepared and have the right mindset.

Many famous actors and comedians still get nervous when they take the stage. Some throw up before speaking to a large crowd, because they are nervous. When the curtain opens and they step out on that stage, they have the right mindset because they've prepared. The confidence they project could be a myth for many who are not really confident. The mindset they project however, is to do the job at hand and they proceed to do so. How do they get into this mindset?

HOW TO USE THE VOICE OF FEAR
Often there's this voice perched on your shoulder, close to your ear that keeps you from having the right mindset. It's the voice of fear that cries out, "Be afraid! Be very afraid!" The voice of fear reminds you to be nervous, to remember your imperfections. While you as an improviser may not be able to cage that bird, you *can* focus elsewhere and ignore its loud voice talkin' smack. You have a job to do. In this instance, the right mindset is to tell that energy of fear-- it has no power over you. Accept that the fear is present, then harness its energy. Tell the fear you are not going to listen to it, because without the facade of confidence, the truth of your being fearful comes forth.

In class, I often state, "Be truthful and do the scene as yourself." That's because many times improvisers try to hide behind a character or caricature. In doing so, either the fear will find you or ego will find you. When you tell fear, it has no power over you because you're not going to hear it squawk, then you are using fear to change your mind set in a positive way. Changing your mindset replaces confidence with completing the task at hand out of a sense of duty and accomplishment. At the same time, changing your mindset takes away fear and ego.

ON STAGE AT SECOND CITY

My first time on stage in an improv show was at Second City, on their L.A. main stage. It was a sold-out house. An early mentor of mine, Tom Booker, currently owner of The Institution Theater, in Austin, Texas and founding member of the Annoyance Theater, in Chicago, was guiding me and several other improvisers without much experience through a scene on stage. Since it was my first time on stage, I stood in the back creating an environment that others could live in. I was furiously making pizza and my object work was superb. At least it felt like it. However, I was nervous.

My spot in the shadows was my safe haven-- that is until Tom spoke to me. Then it all came crashing down. Reality was upon me. I was in the scene. Crap, he's directing dialogue at me. Me... I wanted to melt into the carpet. I was scared. Jumbled thoughts ran through my head. Why was I on stage in the first place? More so, why was I even an improviser, because this is scary! Everything I knew about the world of improv flashed before me. However, I knew Tom Booker had my back. He taught me "trust" that day.

The performance seemed to be moving in slow motion, but actually in an instant, it was over. I survived the scene, and every time after that, it got easier and easier for me to jump on stage and play. I never stopped feeling a little twinge of fear, but I learned to channel it into my work. My mindset was to get the job done, and that's what your focus should be.

I thought to myself, do I have the confidence to do this? No. Am I ready to face my fears? Perhaps. Ready or not, for some insane reason I told myself, I am getting on that stage. It's just about having the right mindset to do the job. Ego is real but it's not going to get you, the improviser, where you want to go. Having the right mindset is.

THE RIGHT MINDSET
Dialing in the right mindset involves telling fear it has no power over you and then blocking that urge to go for the joke. If you do go for the joke, you'll get your laugh, but the scene will be done. There's no longevity and it rarely if ever supports your scene partner. Never go for the joke in improv.

I often laugh a lot. More so because it's freeing but partially it's my job as a comedian to do so. I'm not a stand-up comic but I am still a comedian. That doesn't mean my improv will not carry serious overtones as well as messages of hope and despair. I speak in comedic tones however black the subject matter may be. There are times when committing to comedy is painful when being too passionate squeezes the life out of the subject at hand. Those moments are rare because most improvisers put blocks up before they go that far. Yet it does happen. Having the right mindset though will make it all okay. Having the right mindset erases the need for confidence or the myth of your having confidence and replaces ego with truth.

STRAIGHT MAN

The straight man is a show business term going back beyond the days of vaudeville used to identify the person in a comedy duo who often reacts seriously, often deadpan, to their partners often silly hijinks. Playing the straight man sounds like it's probably easy. It's not. Playing the straight man requires skill. Playing the straight man well, requires special skills. As a character choice the straight man is probably as old as comedy itself. Some improvisers are a natural for playing the straight man in a scene and some have to work at it.

The straight man is the most under-appreciated character in any scene. Most improvisers tend not to gravitate toward playing the straight man. However, the straight man can be the most important character in a scene. Playing the wacky over the top character that interacts with the straight man seems more fun, and it does take skill to do it right-- but not nearly the skill needed to play the straight man correctly.

Though the straight man sometimes works alone, they are often part of a comedy duo. In the duo, one of the comedians gets the laughs and provides ridiculous antics as the wacky off-the-wall character, while the other improviser plays the straight man, also known as "the feed" or "the stooge". The straight man keeps an even keel, reacting reasonably or even serious, in response to the other character's unorthodox, silly antics. The straight man sets up the jokes and feeds them to the comic foil, who gets the laughs as the perpetrator of over the top or unusual behavior. The straight man almost never gets the laughs, with the exception of those garnered from sarcastic reactions or occasional dead pan humor.

On stage, new improvisers gravitate toward playing silly off-the-wall characters. Even though the straight man has what some would argue is the most important role in the comedy duo, it's the more over the top antics that get all the attention-- which is why new improvisers are attracted to playing the comic foil, not the straight man.

Over the years, some dynamic comedy duos with a straight man have included Martin and Lewis, Hope and Crosby, Abbott and Costello, and Desi Arnaz and Lucille Ball in "I Love Lucy". In the UK, exceptional comedy duos with a straight man include Morecambe and Wise, The Two Ronnies, and Wooster and Jeeves. All mentioned have wonderful early footage available to be studied online.

At times, the straight man is not part of a duo. Examples include Margaret Dumont, who as a straight man character always played the blue blood society woman in Marx Brothers films, or Graham Chapman, who would often play the straight man with his Monty Python team members. English actor Stephen Fry is another straight man example.

THE SHORTCUT
In our everyday lives, away from the stage, playing the straight man can happen due to circumstances. Take for example my own infamous "shortcut" ride in a friend's aging Chariot. It was a serious situation with a straight man, namely me, and my friend as the unorthodox cohort who had been driven to that end by circumstance. Perhaps we should have stopped to check the car straight away. That was the thought that crossed my mind, but we hadn't stopped. We just kept driving, though both of us heard the sound. We thought nothing of the sound at first. I did say we… I'm referring to my buddy and fellow musician and band member. He was at the wheel.

A few years later, my buddy would go on to play with a major label rock act that had a Billboard charting single. Though that night my buddy and I were late for a local rock show across town in Los Angeles, which is at least 90 miles across diagonally. We were late and needed a solution. It was also Saturday night and west side traffic was a maze of gridlock.

As we pulled out, I had an epiphany. I'd remembered a little known, less traveled shortcut that would shave us time on our journey, so I shared the info with my buddy who was driving. It was a little-known shortcut I'd discovered the week before, right through the middle of the city. It was a little-known shortcut partly because most folks could not remember where it was, and partly because hardly anyone used it any longer. There was good reason for that. It followed the train's route. The short cut would take us over roads that were fully paved, some that were half paved and some sections that were not paved at all, plus we'd drive over several sets of railroad tracks. None of the proposed route was well lit and we were traveling in darkness. Nevertheless, we crammed ourselves into his fading chocolate brown Ford Maverick for the journey.

"Are you sure you know this shortcut" he asked? Oh sure. I've got this, I assured him. The Maverick was battle tested. It been on the road many years and had seen a lot but was past its prime and on its last legs. Unknowingly I was about to assist with speeding up the process. The shortcut-- now identified as Greg's shortcut, since I had suggested it and would be blamed for anything that went awry-- started out seemingly normal. We drove along a paved road that soon turned to partially paved, then to gravel. By the time we reached the railroad tracks, there were no streetlights, and the bumpy road was an unpaved trail. Then it happened.

STRAIGHT MAN COMES INTO PLAY
Somewhere after the rail crossing there was a "whunk" sound. Though it was loud we ignored it. Maybe we just didn't want to deal with what this sound might be. Eventually we stopped to get our bearings. We were lost. I got out and assessed the situation to discover the Maverick was leaking gas. We decided to abandon the shortcut and had to back up for a mile or so since we couldn't turn around. Eventually we made our way back to lit city streets and completed the trip across town.

Back on paved streets, it sank in that we were leaking gas. That's when my friend became very animated and started to lose it. The shortcut had been a disaster. Since we'd taken the shortcut on my recommendation, I stayed stoic and kept my mouth shut. The quieter I was, the more animated my friend became.

We arrived at the club right on time for the show, thanks to my short-cut. Though I wasn't about to take credit. Outside the venue after the show I examined the Maverick. Yep, we were leaking gas alright.

Patrons were streaming out of the club. Someone stopped and offered me a ride back across town in their car. I thought about it. My buddy heard me get the ride offer and came running over to announce loudly, "You're riding with me! If this car blows up and I die, you're going to die with me!" I wasn't interested in an early grave, but I did feel guilty about my shortcut, so I climbed back in the Maverick for the ride home.

We were not just leaking gas. It was pouring out. Aside from a spark that might cause the car to ignite and burst into flames with us in it, running out of gas was a very real possibility. I stayed straight faced as my friend once again became animated. He was upset which was understandable.

With my head part way out the window I was put on "spark duty" as our gas gauge raced toward empty, like a rocket burning fuel after blast off. There was not just a hole but a large hole in our gas tank and we both knew it. Still, the more animated my buddy became the calmer I became.

The calmer I became, the more of a caricature of himself he became. My friend and band mate had become the unorthodox character of a comedy scene-- and I the straight man. He made sarcastic remarks while flailing his arms about and our conversation now mirrored a scripted comedic scene. However, we both knew there was still the chance of us dying in a fiery explosion.

When should you play the straight man? The rule of thumb is to play the straight man if your scene partner has made an out of the ordinary character choice or taken the scene in an unusual direction. Ask yourself, "What does the scene call for?" In all cases it is imperative that the straight man reacts as ordinary as possible contrasting with the moves and dialogue of the wacky unorthodox character. It's the

129

straight man's job to keep the scene believable while the straight man feeds the unorthodox character lines, looks or subject matter to work off of.

The straight man drives the action and often raises the stakes. It's the straight man who provides continuity and confirms the truth of the scene. When the straight man does his or her job well, the scene looks flawless in the eyes of the audience.

I once played the straight man in a scene that got an exceptional amount of laughs in an improv show. Jesus was on the cross, center stage, and two improvisers were performing a scene in front of him. I was playing Joseph and was offstage. The two improvisers left the stage and I walked on, stopping in front of the crucifixion, then looking up at Jesus on the cross, I simply shook my head, shrugged my shoulders, and walked back off stage. I had no lines. It brought the house down. We performed the piece to numerous audiences as a sketch. People were rolling in the aisles every time. My role was super simple. That scene stood out every time. Learn to play the straight man. It's an invaluable skill.

EXPLORING THE FIRST UNUSUAL THING

To explore the first unusual thing in a scene, the unusual thing must be identified and accepted by both scene partners. Often the improvisers in the scene miss the first, and even the second and third unusual thing in the scene, because they are looking for something weird rather than something unusual or slightly out of the ordinary. Unusual still smells of truth-- and that's important to the improv scene. Remember you are not looking for something crazy or weird but something that might come up in normal conversation that is unusual. You're not out to discover the weirdest thing.

I'm watching an improv scene. The location is a convenience store. The owner is at the counter and a couple enters. The couple are on a long road trip cross country. As the conversation continues and the scene develops, the couple ask for various convenience store items but learn as the audience does that everything in the shop happens to be ingredients for spicy south of the border food and that every ingredient is green.

Picture a convenience store that only sells green south of the border food items and the shop is located in Jersey just off the turnpike, rather than in Texas or New Mexico.

Whenever there is an unusual thing it must be justified in the scene. Turns out that the convenience store owner loves jalapeños, taco fixings and the color green, so that's all his store keeps in stock-- green south of the border food items. The first unusual thing becomes evident as the scene unfolds and the couple inquire about items in the store one by one. They catch on by about the third or fourth item.

THE MENONITE
When my family moved from California to Pennsylvania Dutch country, I dated a sweet Mennonite girl that first summer between junior high and high school. When school started, we went our separate ways, attending different high schools and lost touch. I ran into her during the next school year at a fast food joint, a couple of towns

away. That's when I saw her with a group of girlfriends dressed differently from of the girl I knew. She was dressed in tight jeans, her long nails covered with wild nail polish and her lips saturated in lip gloss. I had to give her a double take. She looked—uh-- different. It was rumspringa.   Now you're thinking, "Uh rumspringa?!" Rumspringa, a Pennsylvania Dutch word, literally translates to running around. As unexpected as it may seem, going through rumspringa is considered a rite of passage for Amish teens. That includes at least some Mennonites too.

Though rumspringa is not a joke, the word itself sounds kind of silly. Audiences might wonder if it's the girl's name. Nope. Is it a term for frost bite? Is it the main character's hunger for anchovies? Since this is a true story and I don't eat anchovies, you can say the third line above is false. Perhaps two is as well. It was high school, and she was on her journey and I on mine. The next time I ran into this girl, she was back in the throes of conservatism and the Mennonite culture. Was rumspringa the first unusual thing?

The first unusual thing could be a California boy dating a Mennonite girl and exploring the differences in culture. The first unusual thing could also be the fast food restaurant that seems to change people, makes them seem sexier, or perhaps it's just the fast food restaurant that is a singles club. Look for concepts that might be slightly unusual. Do not pick an idea to explore that's so crazy you lose the audience. In musical terms, a guitar solo doesn't start on ten. It starts at three or four and builds to ten. I know this. I was a professional musician.

Sometimes the improvisers have to dig a little deeper to uncover the first unusual thing. It doesn't have to be something wild either-- just slightly out of the ordinary. Both improvisers on stage both must agree on what that unusual thing is before proceeding. To do so, both acknowledge simultaneously to one another that they're on the same page, or one improviser makes it clear to the other what the unusual thing is. However, that doesn't always work. In that case, the scene proceeds until the next unusual thing is uncovered, and hopefully the improvisers both see that next one clearly.

Think of the unusual thing as a shiny new penny. Once improvisers agree on what the shiny new penny is, they can play with that shiny new penny, flashing it around in the scene. Each time they come back to that shiny penny; the scene is heightened. Heightening can be achieved by increasing emotion each time the shiny penny appears or approaching the shiny penny from another direction.

Once both improvisers on stage have identified the first unusual thing and agreed that it is the first unusual thing, then they must accept this unusual thing into the world of the scene. This is done by reacting realistically to the unusual thing and justifying the unusual thing in the world of the scene.

AVOIDING CRAZY TOWN

So you've discovered the first unusual thing and both scene partners are in on it. Your next challenge is to explore that unusual thing without going to crazy town--that is, not accepting the unusual thing by causing such weirdness that the scene makes no sense and it ends in a death spiral. In other words, don't allow the scene to get so wacky it goes off the rails-- cause that's a trip to crazy town.

Read the street signs in the scene and avoid crazy town. Crazy town is the scene from hell where everything is weird and there is no connection to any lines of sanity. I'd say, "Do what thou wanteth but thou be prepared to die an ugly death at the behest of thine own hands."

Sometimes improvisers are either afraid to explore the unusual thing or they jump into the muck and just go nuts without taking a moment to observe their surroundings. Remember, the journey to crazy town is quick and destructive. Once the scene has gone there there's practically no salvaging it. So why do it? There are many reasons, from not listening to your scene partner to nervousness. Some improvisers may find getting weird an easy path to walk down. However, inexperience and overreaching in search of something funny are probably the main reasons scenes go to crazy town.

HOMAGE TO MONTY PYTHON

"Can you tell me the way to the ministry of silly walks?!" It's a line of dialogue from a Monty Python sketch that I watched over and over and over in my youth. Just out of high school, my buddies and I would make the 30 minute drive from Pennsylvania Dutch country to New Hope, Pennsylvania, a tourist destination founded in 1939 on the Pennsylvania side of the Delaware River, with one of the oldest summer stock theaters in the country. Art lives in the woods outside Philly…

Up the road from the village of New Hope, we'd pass Peddler's Village, a well landscaped upscale tourist shopping area with a small town feel that's now grown to 40 acres and 60+ shops. Tourists pack the shops to take advantage of tax savings in Pennsylvania, as well as the beauty of the grounds and surrounding woods and streams.

We'd park near Peddler's Village and walk up to groups of tourists that might be standing in front of the quilting shop, or some other random business, and ask in a very calm, proper English accent or character voice we'd emulate the Python lads, "Can you tell me the way to the Ministry of Silly Walks?" The tourists would digest the question and there would inevitably be a long pause. The member of our group who'd asked the question would then waddle, scurry, limp or lumber away in some distinctly odd manner. The tourists would stand stunned, and we would then gather away from the crime and enjoy a belly laugh together. It was all very sophomoric. I enjoyed playing off the strangers.

TRUTH OF THE SCENE

Was the above action an unusual thing or a visit to crazy town? The answer? It was an unusual thing. Though the Ministry of Silly Walks is a silly sounding place, it could just as easily have been the Ministry of Silly Elbow Greetings. Still, we played our roles seriously. It was an action that could be justified in the world of the scene. "Sure, I just dropped my kid at the Ministry of Silly Elbow Greetings. They're offering a course in napkin etiquette and I thought my son could benefit from it." If this were an improv scene we'd have needed to answer "why" there was a need for a Ministry of Silly Elbow Greetings, which would justify its existence in the world of the scene.

There can be more than one unusual thing in the scene. Whether you identify and agree on the first unusual thing or the third, when you do it gives the improvisers a shiny coin to play with-- and that can lead to game, which is another discussion. If the scene partners miss connecting on the first thing, then they should continue the scene with an eye out for the next unusual thing.

THE SNEEZE
In a normal scene, the unusual thing might be a subtle idea. Ask yourself, why use a sledgehammer to crack a walnut? A young man is on a date with his high school sweetheart. They're seated in an upscale restaurant-- well it's as upscale as he can afford. During dinner they are having a normal conversation when he notices that she sneezes whenever he mentions coffee and dessert. She doesn't just sneeze once, but every time he refers to the subject.

The first sneeze is an innocent allergy, but then by the second or third sneeze he decides to explore the sneeze as an unusual thing and see where that leads. The girlfriend's job, once she sees him exploring the sneeze as the unusual thing, is to say "yes and" to his choice. He must agree that she's having an allergy. Later in the scene if the allergy is justified and played seriously, your scene will succeed.

Working with your scene partner, explore, identify, share, justify and heighten in that order… You got this!

PART THREE

SENSE OF URGENCY

When a scene has a sense of urgency it takes on new life. The scene then demands the focus of the audience as it plays out in front of them. Urgency creates cohesion which brings characters and the story line together, as the action unfolds. First the scene must define this day as being important and not just another average day-- then the scene can take on a sense of urgency.

Think about life. There are days when we go about our business and the day merely passes, and there are days when we establish that this day has special merit and we watch the details of the day-- for it is a day that has a sense of urgency.

Once we establish that this day is important, and why it is an important day, we can give this day a sense of urgency. We give the day a sense of urgency by heightening the tensions between the improvisers on stage or ratcheting up other tensions in the scene. Often, it's a need to solve a problem within a specific short time frame.

THE MAGICAL CHAIR

Speaking as an improvisor, I once sold a magical chair to actor Jon Cryer! It was a magical chair of French Provincial design that had belonged to a Hollywood psychic, which was evident in its golden glow as I loaded it into Cryer's SUV. Not everyone could see the glow mind you, yet it was there.

The chair was warm to the touch from the glow, which made the surprise even greater, when Cryer's pregnant wife picked out that particular chair at my yard sale in the Hollywood Hills. Jon stayed in the car so as not to be recognized, perhaps because they were yard sale shopping? Perhaps because his wife, who had already spotted the chair as they were driving by, wanted to be the one to make the purchase. In any event, I loaded it into their SUV. They were pleasant, and the chair was magical.

I'm assuming they discovered my yard sale because they saw my signs...NOT! There were no signs because the neighbors took all our signs down as quickly as I hung them. Yard sales are frowned upon in the Hollywood Hills, or at least the signs themselves are frowned upon. You see-- the signs might draw average city folks from the streets below, and without signs it is hard to find yard sales like ours up in the hills amongst the twists and turns of the winding streets. Aha! Another sign that even without a sign the chair was magical.

Let's talk about the magic of this glowing chair. How do I know the chair was magical you might ask? What proof do I have? A few weeks after selling the chair to Cryer, *Two and a Half Men* debuted on television with Cryer in one of the starring roles. That chair, the one I had sold to Jon Cryer's wife, had brought Cryer success! I'm certain it was a sign of the chair's magic! Never mind that the show had been in production for months previously and the idea, perhaps for years.

What other magic might be a product of the glowing chair? If this were an improv scene, think-- if this is true, then what else is true in the world of the scene? However, this is a true story, right?! Of course, it is. Umm, okay, well most of it is true. Fine, not most, but some of it is true. Yes, I did sell Jon Cryer the chair in question, and his wife did pick it out at my yard sale in the Hollywood Hills. They of course had no idea where it came from, but it did also come from someone quite special. Okay, yes, she was a Hollywood psychic who had passed. However, that's where the truth of the tale ends, or does it?

SENSE URGENCY
You can probably surmise that the above story would make an interesting improv scene. Think about it. A name actor buys this chair which turns out to have a magical golden glow, only visible to those with some special gift for seeing the golden glow. Then suddenly, the actor-- who had been a child star-- is suddenly a star once again. I'm sure Cryer's wife saw the glow, and that's why she purchased it. Oh, back to that again.

I've introduced the concept of a magical chair, which added to the scene that would otherwise just be the sale of a chair at a yard sale. Thus, the day isn't just the day Jon Cryer bought a chair at a yard sale-- it's the day he bought the chair that changed his life. The scene now has a sense of urgency. Today is now an important day. Of course, the audience sees this because in improv it's important to show and not tell.

Magical or not, the chair is an integral part of the above story, adding to what would be an otherwise bland day. In improv we take the concept that has been established, accept it and add something to it, which is "yes and" (as we have described earlier in this book), but now, it's the improvisers job to add something that says "this day is more important than any other day." We've established that this day is now special. The day reeks of importance.

What do we add to make the concept of importance into urgency? A time constraint is one way. Perhaps the chair must be selected by a certain time for its magical glow to recharge from the energy of the right owner, but things keep getting in the way of its rightful owner taking possession, such as the yard sale signs being taken down.

REWIND YOUR DAY
Perhaps you added valuable information to give the scene urgency, but somehow, the scene is still just bland, or at best, sort of important. What is the solution? Look back at the beginning of the scene for clues as to where and how to add urgency. Rewind your time on stage in search of those clues.

Speaking of rewinding, rewinding your day in the world of your daily life can help you prioritize and problem solve, not to mention strengthen your improv scenes with valuable insight as to where scenes were strong and where they went off the rails, and when and how to add urgency to a scene. Rewinding your day is easy, but we seldom even attempt doing so. All you need is five or ten minutes to rewind your day.

CHALLENGE

At the end of the day before bed, turn off the television or stereo and relax for a minute in a comfortable chair. Close your eyes and meditate for a minute or two, relaxing your mind. Next go back to the beginning of your day and tell your mind to play back events of the day. If parts are fuzzy ask your subconscious for clarification. Some parts you may go back over a few times. First, this is a great memory strengthening exercise. Second, you're clearing out your subconscious and making it available. Third, and perhaps the most important, is that rewinding your day is a great way to correct bad habits, improve your outlook on life, and get to know yourself just a little better.

As an improviser you may just want to start by going back over the rehearsal or show that evening. Rewind to the point of your arrival at the rehearsal or show. Look at the details in your mind. How were you feeling? How were others feeling? Were you aware of the energy in the room? What worked and what didn't work for you? For your scene partner? For your team members? Make a few mental notes, tell your subconscious to please remember those notes then release the rewind. Let it go. No matter what you find, positive or negative, thank your subconscious and come back to the present.

Always ask yourself in a scene why is this day more important than any other day? Give the day and your scene a sense of importance and a sense of urgency. Ask yourself, how can you up the stakes? In the paragraph above I didn't just state I sold a chair at a yard sale, but I sold a magical chair!!! I was building the story and adding urgency. I wonder if Jon Cryer and his wife still own the chair? I sat in it many times. Yep, the chair must be magical. Then perhaps I might benefit from its magic all these years later? So why didn't I buy the damn thing?! Oh right, you can't keep every magical chair.

TWO TRUTHS

In improv there are two truths. There is the truth of our everyday lives and the truth of the scene. These two truths live side by side in a multi-dimensional universe. Some truths live in one world or the other and some truths live in both worlds.

Truth in improv is defined as any concept or bit of information accepted as truth in the world of the scene. This includes any unusual concept that might not be accepted in the world of our everyday lives but has been justified in the world of that scene. The concept is justified in the scene when the improvisers on stage show its use and value in that world, and thus accept that concept in the world of the scene as truth. Truth in the world of our everyday lives may or may not be a truth accepted in both the world of the scene and the world of our everyday lives.

I arrived at the Country Store in Malibu for breakfast, early on a Sunday morning. Composer Danny Elfman was seated on the porch. You've heard Elfman's music in *The Nightmare Before Christmas, Justice League, Men in Black International, Fifty Shades of Grey* and many others. His composing talent is genius. I hadn't seen him for at least twenty years, so I'm sure he didn't recognize me from all those years ago. People were arriving and his sanctum-sanctorum was no longer in place. Elfman left soon after.

When last our paths had crossed, Elfman was leading the band Oingo Boingo. Their press machine and possibly the group's management had been peppering the music world with perceived truths which they hoped would become accepted truths. As the band shaped their narrative for fans, there was a narrative the powers that be did want audiences to embrace and one they didn't want audiences to embrace. Not because one was bad, but because one did not play into the narrative the publicist spun for the public. Neither effected their music.

When on stage in improv anything that happens in the world of the scene-- if played as though you are living in that world 24-7-- will eliminate any need to differentiate between the two worlds. Your commitment and belief in, or response to, the truth happening on stage will make that truth so powerful it will transcend both worlds.

If you're not a film buff or fan of 90's alternative rock or new wave, perhaps you're not familiar with either Danny Elfman or Oingo Boingo. Danny Elfman's big composing break came when Director Tim Burton discovered his band, liked their tunes, and asked Elfman to write the music for the film *Pee Wee's Big Adventure.*

Elfman was hesitant at first, since he had no formal training, but Boingo guitarist Steve Bartok, who had been trained in scoring, assisted. The pairing of Elfman with Burton paid off. In improv we call that daring to fail. Take chances! Move the story and thus the scene forward. Strengthen your weakest skills by taking chances, work those mental muscles and try new things. Danny Elfman stepped into the composing role with passion.

The Mystic Knights of the Oingo Boingo, Elfman's first ensemble, were street performers doing a mixture of circus sideshow activities including juggling, acrobatics, sword swallowing, and cabaret music. Their show was improvised performance art, delivered spontaneously on the Venice, California boardwalk.

The night Oingo Boingo had their major label debut it took place at the Whisky-a-go-go in West Hollywood, California. It was the culmination of years of work. I was with them, and for me it was the completion of an article on the band I'd written, after weeks of research and meeting with band members at their rehearsal space. I had become friends with the sax player.

Oingo Boingo had two truths. There was the actual truth about the band's background including members' credits and philosophies, and there was the truth that Elfman and management wanted audiences to accept. Truth versus projected truth. The projected truth now be their truth for many of those in attendance. Which would it be?

After collecting my credentials at the box office, I entered the club and climbed the stairs to show my pass to security on the second-floor balcony. I then passed through a door to a second set of stairs toward the Whisky-a-go-go green room, located up over the club. The green room is where the performers gather before their shows to stretch and tune up and bask in their pseudo local stardom. On this night, the activity in the green room was about serious preparation before taking the stage for the show.

As I walked into the green room, I spotted Danny Elfman on the floor in gym shorts, doing sit-ups, deep knee bends and stretches to loosen up, which was a far cry from the band's arty rebel street image. We nodded hello to one another. I spoke with some of the players then left as they continued to warm up. Back in the audience I spied the entire A&M records upper echelon nestled along the balcony at small tables. They were patiently waiting for Oingo Boingo to take the stage and to experience a taste of their investment.

Up until this point, the Oingo Boingo show had been a visual experience perfecting French cabaret tunes and vaudeville moves coupled with something otherworldly and theatrical. Oingo Boingo were now a full-fledged rock act yet they still wanted the public to see them as artsy and street. Their roster now included session musicians with credits as varied as Tom Jones and Aretha Franklin brought in to flesh out the band. However, keeping those secrets seemed important to the band's leader.

What was their actual truth now? Here's where the definition gets interesting. Their actual truth was whatever the audience that night experienced in the club and walked away with in their heart. The audience discovered the music and accompanying stage show as it unfolded. Therefore, what the audience and the artists discovered together that night was the actual truth of the scene.

Two truths. The truth of the world of your everyday life and the truth of the world of the scene. Sometimes one and the same and sometimes not. Concepts that are justified in the scene, played seriously, and received seriously, are accepted in the world of the scene as truth. They've been given purpose in that world. Play your scenes truthfully and justify the unusual. And somewhere between the two worlds you'll find the funny. It exists in the truth of the scene.

WHY IS THIS DAY SPECIAL?

There are days that blend into one another and there are days that you remember for years, some for a lifetime. Those are the days that have been defined as special. Think what makes this day special, what sets it apart? You don't have to burn your business to the ground to have a special day at work. Perhaps today is the day that you had your first customer because you just opened to the public or perhaps it's your 100,000th customer or it's the day your dog ate that pizza your boss ordered. Oops! Why did you bring your dog to work anyhow?!

Now urgency sets the scene on fire and there may be an urgent matter to attend to but any small thing that makes this day special is just as good when kicking off a scene. When entering a scene always think; "What makes this day special?"

In improv, to give the scene legs, to heighten the action, we must define why today is important. "You're late for the third time this week Martha," is an important detail in telling the story of the scene, but by using specificity, we can tighten the focus on Martha's behavior.

Just adding one detail heightens why this day is important. "You're late for the third time this week Martha, and you know the Times food critic is coming to review us this morning!" Now we know she's not just late again, but she's been late three times in one week, and in doing so, she's letting down her employer.

Looking at our everyday lives there are days that scream with importance, and some that could use an added detail to give the scene importance and add that sense of urgency. What elements make this day important? The answer is-- any action that elevates the scene's heart rate makes this day important.

A DAY IN BEIRUT
Beirut, Lebanon was once a premiere vacation destination in the Middle East and a seat of culture. Its downtown streets were teaming

145

with the beauty of fashion, art and an amalgam of religious groups. The city was decimated in the 1970s but over the years has made its way back and though it has had its setbacks, is a tourist destination once more.

I was going through a box of keepsakes in mom's closet when I came across a heavy room key from a hotel, the Intercontinental Hotel Phoenicia in Beirut, Lebanon. The key looked as though it had been hand made in a forge. Not your average room key. I studied the heavy piece of memorabilia, remembering that Dad had been in Lebanon on business when I was in high school.

Dad traveled a lot as I was growing up. He would often leave for weeks at a time. I enjoyed the postcards or money from unusual places. Dad was short on the phone but would call just about every day. Mom would wait patiently in our Pennsylvania Dutch farmhouse for that daily call. Cornfields and sheep surrounded our house in the country. There was also the occasional flutter of a pheasant spooked by hunters. Though Philadelphia was only an hour or so away, it seemed like another world from us.

So far, we have an average day, an average week and a trip, average on its face, though it's a trip to a foreign land, which is a far cry from my high school years in Pennsylvania Dutch country, but still non-eventful. In improv we examine the concept of why this day is more important than any other. When we examine what makes this day important in life, it may help us decipher what elements are needed in the world of the scene to achieve that same goal.

THE BATTLE
The phone rang. It was Dad calling from the Phoenicia Hotel in Beirut, Lebanon. On our end, in Pennsylvania Dutch country, it was a quiet evening as the sun was setting over our farmhouse. I answered the phone. Dad seemed tense as he asked for Mom. I stayed on the extension to listen in. Intermittent noise on the other end of the phone

forced him speak even louder than usual. You could hear the long-distance line fading and he seemed distant.

I could now make out a loud noise. It was in the background. A loud popping that came and went. Dad told Mom it was the clatter of machine gun fire that was rattling on in the background. The sound would stop and start and ran in bursts. I was naive to the danger. As a kid I thought, "What an exciting situation." Dad not so much. I guess I'd spent too much time in the corn fields of Pennsylvania Dutch country.

Now if this were a scene, I'd have established that this day now is not only important, but that it has urgency. The scene has established that this day has life and death importance. Establishing the day as being an important one helps the characters solidify an emotional connection, and thus gives the improvisers on stage a chance to get on the see-saw between normalcy and heightening the action, and to ride that see-saw. In real life, the emotional connection could be felt over the phone.

Dad explained that he'd been gathered up with a group of Brits and was about to be taken down to the lobby. He hoped they'd evacuate him with the Brits. Dad told Mom he loved her and that he'd stay on the call as long as possible-- which turned out to be only a few minutes. Dad knew it could be his last call. I was a kid and kids do and say dumb stuff. I said that all the action sounded cool. He said it wasn't. It was dangerous. Dad was scared. I'd never known Dad to be scared ever. He told Mom he'd get back to her as soon as possible.

Throughout the evening the fighting increased outside the hotel. We didn't have cable news, so it was hard to follow as events unfolded. One thing that made the news was that fighting had broken out and that Westerners were being evacuated. We later learned that Dad had managed to leave with the last of the Brits.

Shortly thereafter, the Hotel Phoenicia, where dad had called us from, was caught between the crossfire of several rebel factions and was burned to the ground in what became known as "the battle of the hotels". That battle outside Dad's hotel was the event that kicked off the Lebanese civil war, a war that raged for 15 years, destroying much of what was once a beautiful country and a cultural destination for travelers.

WHAT DOES MAKE THIS DAY SPECIAL?

In Improv, the most interesting scenes visually tell the audience why this day is special and what makes it stand out from any other day. They also have a sense of urgency which the improvisers share.

In the above story it's easy to tell why that day was important. In improv we have to create situations making the day that the scene takes place an important day. Of course, most are not life and death challenges. When a scene takes place on a day that's important and it's clear to the audience why the day is important, and what sets that day apart from every other, the audience is with you.

Always think: what makes this day special? Remember to show it, don't tell it. Think: what can I add to give the scene importance? What details might make this day stand apart from any other day? "Uh-oh here comes that angry mob. Glad I'll be sharing the storm cellar with you. We just need to load all these supplies...Damn it, I can't find the key. I guess I should have made that extra copy last week at the hardware store."

IMPROV WANTS

An average character carrying no emotion and without a want is a bland character about to have a boring scene. It's important for your character to have a want. What does your character want and how do you determine that want?

We have wants in our everyday lives, so why not on the improv stage? In our everyday lives there is the over-arching want to have a happy and healthy life. There's also the over-arching want to be loved. It could be as simple as having someone in our lives to share hugs with. There is the daily want for a successful trouble-free day. There is the situational want of a good meal, or to sign a new client, or to make satisfying art, or just to get through the rest of the day without hunger or health issues.

A SINGLE DRIVING FORCE
In improv you can measure wants as the single driving force an im-proviser's character brings to the scene. You can walk into the scene with a want, or your character can develop the want in the scene-- which is more work. If your want is strong enough, your scene partner will be forced to deal with that want on an emotional level. That's a good thing. Remember, in improv the scene is about the relationship, and the want drives that relationship.

Children have strong wants. Usually they are simple wants but still very powerful. That's one of the reasons it's so rewarding to play as a child. An improviser's want can change during the scene. In the world of your everyday life you may have many wants, and all at the same time that coexist throughout your day. In the world of the improv scene it's best to pick one or two to invest energy in. Take a moment and look at your life. Pick a couple of situations and identify the wants. They're usually just under the surface.

AT AGE 8 / THE BIG BUZZ
At age 8 my family was living in Houston, Texas. It was a time when the suburbs of the southwest were filled with the buzz of mosquito

herds. Sundown and sunrise were particularly treacherous. The mosquitoes were thick.

My young buddies and I would lie in wait for the evening pest control truck, the one that would spray copious amounts of DDT based poison to kill all the mosquitoes. We were commandos, brave undercover fighters with our imaginary weapons in hand and oblivious to the effects of the clouds sprayed on the populace. I always wondered why no one was out at that time. Hmmm.

Lying in wait as though preparing for a raid, we'd run through the thick smoke that trailed behind the mosquito truck weaving in and out in it. Holding my imaginary weapon at the ready, we'd charge, making battle cries. What was our want? Perhaps it was adventure. Perhaps intrigue. Maybe just to create fond memories that would lead to work on Hollywood film set years later, or on the flip side, it created an asthmatic issue I'd be addressing as a grownup. We were 8-year-old shirtless warriors of the southwest! Our characters in the moment had wants!

In the above story we had simple, strong wants. Those wants filled our characters and defined the scene. Remember, the more specific and personal the want, the more intense and interesting the scene.

AT AGE 11 / AMAZING KRESKIN DELIVERS
At age 11 my homeroom teacher administered the Amazing Kreskin ESP board game as a test, to a handful of students willing to pass on recess. I was one of them. It was a tough choice, but the intrigue of playing the Kreskin mentalist game kept me in my seat.

My teacher, determined to flesh out any "closet psychics," administered the test. After the first round of play, a small group of us remained. During the second round, my ears turned to the sounds coming from the playground outside the classroom, and my answers didn't stand up to the teacher's scrutiny. I was excused. I arrived on the playground just in time to enjoy half a recess.

I had several wants. One was to feel accomplished, two was to be deemed special amongst the class members, and as the scene unfolded, a third want was to feel the asphalt beneath my feet during recess! Wants connect characters to the scene. The greater the connection between characters, the greater the scene.

If you think back on your childhood, there will be stories that stand out and with each story you recall, you can probably name at least one clear want.

AT AGE 12 / THE PHARAOH'S WRATH
At age 12, a teacher of mine had an Egyptian display on the bulletin board near the front of the classroom. He had spent quite some time putting the display together with pictures, lettering, and colored paper cut outs shadowing the images. An unnamed student (not I) had taken pins to the eyes of the Pharaohs, poking them all out. Soon an Egyptian anthropological display had been transformed into a horror film story board.

The teacher was angry. No one fessed up. Though I don't remember the punishment, I know we all paid the price. My teacher had the strongest want, which was to uncover the culprit. He tried for weeks. It was an Agatha Christie moment.

When there is a strong want, the other characters' wants sometimes become secondary, as they play off the character with the stronger desire. Whenever we lined up to go outside by the bulletin board, I had to stifle a laugh, though I did feel sorry for my teacher.

AT AGE 13 / BIRTH CURSE OF LEAP YEAR
At age 13, my family was living in Orange County, California, about an hour south of Los Angeles. Being that leap year comes once every four years, and I was born on a leap year, the local paper thought a general story about that birthdate would be of interest, and I would be in the story.

A reporter and photographer came to our house. The photographer took pictures of me blowing out candles. I wanted to look cool. When the photographer started snapping pictures, I made a face, which much to my chagrin, graced the front page of the next day's newspaper. It was a close-up. I had a sour look on my face as though I'd just eaten a batch of bad yogurt. At thirteen I didn't find the process "cool," so I hadn't cooperated.

The reporter had a strong want which was to do the assignment and get paid. My want was to look cool. Uh what happened? Oh right, I made a face. When two characters have strong wants that are not in sync, there is conflict in the scene and often clear comedic results. The comedic photo on the front page of the local paper was at my expense and was the result of a strong want. Maybe I should have thought that one through a bit more...

You can see, in our everyday lives we all have wants. Every character in every scene has a want whether you take the time to identify that want before going into the scene or not. However, a well-defined want in the scene will help the scene.

Remember that the audience has wants as well. They want to discover our wants and they want to be entertained-- whether they laugh or not. It's not always about the laughter in improv. It's about being playful and building interesting worlds. Be interesting and have a want.

CHALLENGE 1
Spend a day identifying your wants in each situation you encounter. Keep a simple list that you can refer back to. If others have strong wants that you have identified, then list those as well. Later you can look at the list to get ideas for possible improv scene wants.

CHALLENGE 2
This is an exercise dealing with wants. It's a two-person scene where each improviser gets a suggestion of a secret want, one that no one else hears except that improviser. Then the two improvisers are to

have a normal scene but play the scene through the lens of the want. Wants can be as varied as: wanting to rule the world, seeing everyone and everything in life as a possible pet, or wanting to be a vampire.

You should attempt to give subtle hints as to your character's secret want, being careful not to be so blatant as to give away the identity of what your secret want is. For example, perhaps your character thinks they are a vampire. Instead of stating "I want to suck your blood," be subtle and maybe say, "I'm starving. Steak sounds good. Very rare…" or, "I prefer we meet in the evening. I'm more of a night owl these days," instead of something telling like "Day time is out of the question. I'll be asleep in my crypt." Be subtle and be honest in how you play your want.

ENDOWING

Endowing is assigning attributes to another improviser's character. To do so is a good thing when it helps the other improviser establish that character (and of course if it is accepted by the other improviser). Smart improvisers endow their scene partners with attributes that also kick the scene into high gear early, increasing the action, and that grabs the audience's attention.

Often a scene will start, and one improviser will endow the other with a physical ailment. "Sam, you've had that limp for quite some time…" Now of course Sam has to remember to limp from that moment forward. Of course, Sam can return the favor and endow his scene partner, "Well Clem, at least I didn't lose an eye in the accident."

Endowing a character with a type of awareness or mental attribute can be just as effective as endowing characters with a limp from an accident or, on the opposite side of the spectrum, endowing them with superhuman traits. The more believable the endowment is, the easier it is for the audience to accept the improvisers using those endowments in the scene. We endow others in our everyday lives as well.

A YANK IN THE DEEP SOUTH

We drove down to the edge of the Georgia swamp, where everyone got out of the car. There was an eerie silence that swept over the calm waters. Our guide was a local boy who gave me the nod. "This is the spot. It's okay to swim here." All eyes were on me. I walked to the water's edge. *Would he, or wouldn't he?* It was apparent that's what they were thinking. I saw it written on their faces. It was time to put up or shut up.

My angels were working overtime. I would be okay; the local boy had told me as much. I chewed on the words as they passed through my brain. He'd given me the nod. Imaginary, protective armor is what he'd shared with that nod. Everyone's eyes were upon me as I slipped into the syrupy water. It smelled of bark and had a reddish tint. My cut-off jeans were tight and man, was I glad they were. No creatures were going to swim up them paint legs I thought, as I swam around a few stumps, gingerly.

"Isn't anyone else coming in?" No one answered. Was I experiencing a rite of passage for locals, or had I, the lone "Yank", been had? Thinking back, who knows how many snapping turtles, gators, snakes and water born pests may have been waiting in the depths to sink their teeth into my flesh. None of that mattered then because I was protected. Our guide had endowed me with the powers of protection, and I accepted his word as fact. Today I look back at swimming in a swamp in horror…

The above story with endowments makes my character exempt from harm. Had it been an improv scene, my character was protected. More specifically, my character had been endowed with the specifics of protection that very day. M. Night Shyamalan often endows characters in his movies and uses the premise from those endowments to build the film around. Don't be afraid of sharing endowments. In our everyday lives we endow one another with traits without even thinking about it. "You were always the smart one" or, "I could not have gotten my car started without your help. You're a mechanical genius." "You're so creative." "Nice to know my roommate is a human calculator." We are not even aware that we are endowing others. Of course, we do so negatively as well.

Should an improviser in a scene find themselves the recipient of unintentionally being endowed--embrace the endowment and utilize it in the scene. "Speaking of my being a human calculator, I just added up all the ants in that colony outside your front door. Based on the stream leaving your windowsill, which I've multiplied by how many fit in a typical colony below ground, you might want to call an exterminator." The character goes on to calculate other random items as the scene moves forward. Endowing is a fun tool.

HOW DOES YOUR CHARACTER FEEL?

When two improvisers are on stage and the scene is merely inching forward or worse, the scene is frozen in place, it's not a good sign-- especially when the scene partners are not relating to one another, which means they're also not heightening the action. If you make the scene about how you feel about your scene partner, you can refocus that energy, and move the scene forward.

I was chatting with a friend about an upcoming trip and the conversation turned to her fear of flying. She knew she was missing out on life and its adventures since she had been unable to fly. I remembered an interesting flight that I was on and reiterated the adventure to her to illustrate a point. It was an emotionally driven story. Great improv is often emotionally driven.

What is emotion? The dictionary says it's a natural instinctive state of mind deriving from one's circumstances, mood or relationships with others. Feelings are the emotional side of one's character. Where do these emotions or feelings come from? Emotions result from the brain, heart and body, acting in concert. The truth is-- emotions are physical and feelings are mental, so actual feelings can't be measured precisely. Many people use the words emotion and feelings interchangeably. Wherever they come from, they carry weight in a scene. Use them. Once again, I ask you, "How does your character feel?" Sometimes what should be a routine activity like flying turns out to be much more.

THE FLIGHT
Seated in an aisle seat, I closed my eyes for a second as the plane left the ground. I felt something attach to my left arm. Opening my eyes, I slowly turned. A petite French woman was seated to my left and she was clutching my arm, evidently terrified as we took off. Once in the air she apologized. I'd heard about passengers that were uncomfortable flying, so I attempted to convince her that everything was fine. As the flight continued and we climbed higher, beads of sweat

appeared on her forehead. She seemed a bit more than just uncomfortable flying. I felt bad for her but still closed my eyes attempting to drift off to sleep.

I sat up when I once again felt something gripping my arm. The higher we flew, the more my arm became a comfort object for the panic-stricken woman. The French woman's make-up began to run as she continued to perspire. Soon she was not only clinging to my arm, but she was doing so with such force that her nails went right through my shirt sleeve and began to dig into it my flesh. It hurt. I thought, okay, nap time is over.

I called the flight attendant over to get water for her, and soon she was not only clutching my arm but holding my hand in a sweaty embrace, her fingers laced in mine. Attempts at napping were now replaced with my focus on soothing her nerves. We shared soft chit-chat of the mundane while I attempted to keep my distance-- as though it would do any good. Her fraught nerves brought on acid reflux and her sweet French voice smelled of vomit. Thank god it was a short flight! When we finally landed, the woman wiped the sweat from her brow, cleaned up her smeared makeup and finally let go of my arm. Thankfully they weren't teeth marks. I was relieved she wasn't a biter. As we began to deplane, she stopped in the terminal, and looking like a nightclub chanteuse at close of business, she addressed me in a breathy French accent asking if I'd like her number. I smiled, knowing that flight was our passing moment and our emotional embrace. Lovely, but a bit too needy, I thought. We never spoke again.

Your character must be able to connect with your scene partner on an emotional level. How does your character feel? How do you feel about what has been said? How do you feel about what is going on around you and about the inner turmoil in your mind and in your heart? After you ask yourself how you feel, know that there is still room for funny. At this point you might be questioning yourself. It doesn't feel funny, it feels uh, emotional. That's okay. The funny will come on its own, and though it would be great if your character reaches for deep rich emotions in your responses, it's not mandatory for great improv.

The story didn't sway my friend to try air travel, but it did turn the thought of air travel from a shiver to a chuckle in her mind. It was clear that my friend could imagine herself in the role of the anxious flyer. If you ask yourself how you feel you'll never run out of things to say, because you always feel something.

METHOD MAN

I met Wu-Tang Clan's Method Man in a comic store. He'd written a graphic novel. I paid homage. We chatted and I posed to have my photo taken with him. Method Man did everything in his power to make me feel at home. It was all very cool, but I for some reason couldn't relax, couldn't let go and couldn't let myself be in the moment. The photo we took together showed me looking very uncomfortable. How I felt was how the photo turned out. I should have embraced the moment, but I did not.

As an improviser there is no right or wrong, but if I'd just been in the moment and emotionally available, I'd still have that picture today. I chatted with his kind wife before and after. What a sweet lady. She knew I was uncomfortable. I shouldn't have been. At that moment I thought-- I'm too old. You are never too old! You are as old as you feel. I wasn't honest with myself about how I felt. My short scene with Method Man could have been a better scene. In life just as in improv we often forget to check in with ourselves. If I'd only asked myself how I felt before posing for the photo with Method Man...

How do you determine what feelings you're having or what feelings you should address in the scene? Just answer the last thing said to your character. Answer honestly. Perhaps your scene partner just said, "You're grounded!" That either establishes you as a parent or a consenting couple with an unusual relationship. Unless of course you are an alien child that can travel between worlds. In that, you're grounded takes on a whole new meaning.

Bring the scene to your scene partner. "Okay mom. I know I stayed out too late again last night but this time we really were studying! When I ace the test, you're going to be proud." Remember, it's not about you, it's about the person you are sharing the stage with. Let your scene partner's words affect you. Ask yourself, how does your character feel about what's just been said?

SHORT STATEMENTS

Make short statements that demand an emotional response in your improv scenes! One simple statement can change a whole scene. One simple word can change the scene as well. No lengthy pointless chatter --and let your scene partner speak! New improvisers often want to share a monologue rather than make a statement, zip it up and let their scene partner speak. They just keep talking. Breathe, and then let the scene breathe. Give and take focus. Often the continued talking is the product of nerves. That's the improviser hoping that if they keep talking, they will say something witty or brilliant, or at least dig themselves out of a dull scene.

HAVING A BAD DAY
I pulled up to the four-way intersection. A flatbed truck had pulled up to the same light, from the feeder road to my right. A late model black sedan rested comfortably on the flat bed. The side windows of the sedan were smashed out and written with spray paint in large pink letters across the entire side of the car, was the word "CHEATER!!!" Someone is not having a very good day I thought.

In improv, making short statements that demand an emotional response will strengthen your status in the scene and hold the audience's attention. That one word sprayed on the side of the car in the above observation was a powerful statement. In improv, short statements go hand in hand with why this day is more important than any other. In other words, what is happening on this day that gives this scene urgency? What is happening that ups the stakes and that connects the two scene partners on a personal level? Once again, I stared at the car on the flatbed truck and all I could think of was, damn! Now that's a powerful short statement and one that demands an emotional response. Lots of scenes in life end with some drama.

However, statements that demand an emotional response don't have to be extreme. As I was mulling this all over in my brain, the light turned green and I moved on to the next scene unfolding for me that morning. Short statements also give both scene partners time to take in what's been said, as they give and take focus. Short statements that connect with your scene partner move the scene forward by giving both scene partners tools to assist as you invest in your characters strong feelings.

IN THE HOSPITAL

My mother was in the hospital for an operation. A day later she had to have an NG tube inserted through her nose down her throat and into her stomach. The night before, the staff had put it in twice, but Mom pulled the tube out twice. I explained the purpose of the tube to Mom and what the doctor was hoping for as a result. Still, to put the tube back was a grand affair. Since it was a grand affair there was not a lot of talking going on. Action was needed, not talking. There were five of us standing over Mom as I snapped my surgical gloves into place and to put it mildly, there was a lot of commotion.

Meanwhile, Mom's very short hospital roommate, came out of the bathroom, and with a fifth nurse guiding her, began to shuffle past Mom's bed. As she reached the foot of Mom's bed, she stopped and proceeded to announce in a loud voice, "I see you are all having a cocktail party!" It was a short statement. Just a few words. Even with all the commotion that was going on that one simple line caused everyone to stop. There were stifled chuckles as the woman shuffled away. Her statement was an example of the power of short statements that demand an emotional response in action. We often think we need to say a bunch of words when all that's needed is a short precise statement. Her statement wasn't heavy either. It was just an observation.

On stage, to make your short statement even more powerful, start in the middle of the action. Now, don't just introduce yourself to your scene partner, "Very nice to meet you. Do you come here often?" Treat the scene as if there was a before and something has just happened, giving your scene importance. "The credit card bill arrived, and I opened it while in line at the bank!" With the latter statement you've just lit a fire under the characters and turned the heat up a notch. Your job is to make sure something important has just happened or is happening. If you do not, you will lose your audience. Polite scenes are boring and almost as bad as wacky crazy town outings. Avoid "boring!"

IN THE LIVING ROOM

Sometimes the short statement can be just one word or the one-line response to that word. I was sitting on my couch in the living room staring at a note on the coffee table. On the note there was one word in the upper left and then a list of things to do around the house written higher up on the paper and to the side-- away from the lone word. I glanced at the note from where I was seated but couldn't quite make out the lone word. I tried to pronounce it out loud, "dah-core-aht-tay". Hmmm. I tried several other pronunciations before asking, "Is it a drug?" My wife seated on the other side of couch looked in my direction, "You've been visiting the hospital too often," which was in reference to my mother, who'd been hospitalized for seven days. It was a short simple statement that demanded an emotional response. "Dah-core-aht-tay," I repeated and laughed. The one word in the left corner was "decorate", written in cursive.

Next time you are in a scene, consciously make short statements. Here are a few: "Your water lilies spoke this morning", "Your mother is coming for dinner, I'm going out!", "I can see by the expression on your face you are not enjoying the lecture.", "I can't believe you feel asleep in (church, temple etc.) again this week. I posted it on Instagram", "If you really cared about me, you'd go to visit my parents for a full weekend." The short statements can be positive as well. "I've always enjoyed watching you paint" or using more specific details, "I've studied every brush stroke of your masterpiece with a magnifying glass." As you master making short statements, you'll add details, which is great. "You stood in the doorway clutching the worn stuffed bear from your childhood and I could swear he was yearning to speak." This will improve your scene work listening skills.

CHALLENGE 1

Have you ever driven through the Midwest or Deep South with miles of nothing except billboards alongside the highway? They're often advertising not only products but places to stop, just off the next exit. Think of those billboards as short statements that demand an emotional response. Look at the images on the billboards with little or no words, and see them as statues, art, or object work in need of a verbal label. Come up with a short phrase or even just a word or two to go with each one. As you pass billboards with lots of copy (printed words) read them out loud. Next, give the phrase you just read a descriptive title in hopes of getting an emotional response that fits with the image. Bet you didn't know you were an advertising professional!

CHALLENGE 2

This is an awareness exercise in addition to putting the concept of making short statements that demand an emotional response to work. Your challenge is to consciously make every statement that comes out of your mouth for a period of time short and to the point, whenever you address someone. Be succinct. In other words, you'll make a conscious effort to monitor what you say for a predetermined period of time. The goal during that time is to only make short, to the point statements. This challenge will be especially helpful for those who can't seem to speak without spewing forth a monologue or soliloquy.

Start with five minutes, then ten minutes, then fifteen minutes, etc. as you get comfortable with the exercise. You'll eventually build your brain in that area and will naturally think about what you say before you speak. After the exchange, think about where the scene could go. Start a list and jot down your ideas.

KEEP THE SCENE PLAYFUL

After a pro-sports team lifestyle brand shoot in Los Angeles, the Director of Photography on the shoot was invited to a roof top party where celebrities were in attendance. Actor Jamie Fox agreed to take a couple of personal snapshots with the DP. As they posed together, the DP asked a woman nearby to take the photo. She declined. Confused that maybe she didn't hear him or misunderstood, he asked again politely, and she once again said no. Later that night, the DP was enjoying the stars from the rooftop and saw the woman. He asked once more, only this time to take a photo of him alone. Once again, she said no. Curious, he asked her why she wouldn't snap a shot of him, and she just said, "I don't do that." Turns out, the woman was a famous pop star who evidently doesn't like not being recognized and deemed taking photos of others to be non-star-like.

A man parks his Porsche outside a coffeehouse in east Hollywood, California. He enters the Indie coffeehouse and orders a cappuccino from the barista. The barista says, "You look like that rock singer in the band…" The man ordering the coffee cuts him off and says, "That's funny, I often get confused for him. However, I work construction." The man who ordered at the register, gets his coffee and sits in a far corner, where another man joins him for coffee. When they finish, the man who first claimed to be a construction worker walks back up to the barista at the register. "Yes, I am a rock singer. My name is Anthony (Keidis) and I am the lead singer for the Red Hot Chili Peppers. It's nice to make your acquaintance."

Two celebrity encounters; two totally different reactions. They both happened as described. I know, because someone close to me was at the first encounter and I was seated by the register for the second encounter. How we relate to others has a bearing on our lives. The first interaction is not playful and one of the characters comes off cold. The second story has a light playful feel and the reader walks away with a smile. We want to keep our scenes playful whenever possible.

We spend so much time ensuring improv scenes make sense that they're often mired in boring dialogue. Other times improvisers are so focused on finding the funny in the scene, that the scenes get so weird, they're abrasive and unpleasant. As an improviser, it's easy to forget that the improv process is about being playful and having fun.

SPARKLEWEIG

What is Sparkleweig? Depends who you ask. Perhaps Sparkleweig is a dance move or maybe a fruity wine, a board game played in the living room or on the lawn, a vegan substitute for pickled fish or the last name of a former boss you had hoped to forget but was just reminded of at dinner. Sparkleweig could also be a town just outside of Amsterdam. Oh right; it is. It's a suburb, a stop on the Metro line…the very clean Danish metro line. Sounds like it was someone's name. Maybe it still is that too. The thing is, you don't know what Sparkleweig is, so why not get playful and have fun with your choice. When improvisers are having fun on stage their scene will be successful!

We often get suggestions we don't know what to do with. If you realize that in improv, the suggestion of Sparkleweig or any other suggestion you accept, can be anything or anyone you want. *"Good morning Mrs. Sparkleweig, nice hat!"* We are taught to think in linear thought patterns. We don't have to do that either. *"Damn it, a little Sparkleweig on the neighbor's yard and I always get blamed!"* Or, *"Sorry I'm late, I stopped for a little Sparkleweig on the way home, and one thing led to another. I believe I overslept!"*

Let a suggestion be anything you want even if you know nothing about what that suggestion is in the existence of your everyday life. In making such an odd choice for a suggestion, you can be playful with it. As grown-ups, we often think, "I don't know what that is" or "I don't understand that topic." Let it exist in the scene as whatever you choose. Let your scene and your dealing with the subject of that scene be playful!

Life, like the scene, has playful moments as well. Pointing them out to ourselves can help improvisers live in the playful moments of their everyday lives. I called my ninety-one-year-old mother who was in the hospital to check on her. "Hey mom what are you doing?" "I'm watching." She replied. "Oh, what show?" "I'm not watching television I'm watching the clouds." Then I remembered her in her apartment looking out at the clouds previously. I arrived at the hospital and joined her-- looking out at the clouds from the large window in her room. There they were-- like unruly teens running about, hiding and reappearing, shape shifting and dancing in groups. A few were even making love. The sky was delivering a playful aria of picturesque formations and characters.

Back in the world of the scene, don't beat your head against a pole and make the scene hard. Have fun with the scene. Be playful! Let's say you are given a serious topic and in the format you are working, you have to create a world around that topic. You've just been given the suggestion *Inner Stellar Space,* and you have little knowledge of the science of inner stellar space-- so you improvise. Make something up and commit to it. It's okay to be light and silly. *"Commander, we've discovered inner stellar space is the world within worlds that thrives in a test tube. We'll be shrinking down and flying across it momentarily."* That was kind of playful?! Wasn't it? Don't forget to use all your senses!

Discover your own Sparkleweig. It lives in all of us. It could be a magical place, an elixir of life or a magical word that opens a gateway to multiple dimensions. And when you do, serve it up playfully. Sparkleweig-- the phrase for "I don't know what that is…"

Keep your improv playful! Make your improv scenes a place you want to return to-- over and over….Sparkleweig! It's a fun word to say and you can mold it into anything you can shape in your mind. Why? Because it's improv. Get creative. Justify and smile. Sparkleweig! Sparkleweig! Sparkleweig!

GROUP MIND

"When the rational mind is shut off, we have the possibility of intui-tion." – Viola Spolin (Acting coach, influenced first generation Second City actors in Chicago in the 1950s)

It takes intuition and observation for group mind to flower. Rational mind, which Spolin eludes to above, I define as corporate thought processes encouraging a hierarchy consciousness as the accepted group etiquette. Group mind as an improv concept, operates in the intuitive realm of the empathic.

I sat down to have dinner with entrepreneur Tim Walsh, a man with an inert sixth sense for identifying patterns and numbers which he uses in the development of board games. The conversation soon turned to Group mind or Group think.

First what is Group mind? If you've been an improviser for any length of time, you've heard of the term and possibly seen it in action. Why is Group mind important? In the world of improv Group mind or Group think is when the individuals that make up a group work together, operating as one voice, developing their own group consciousness.

Group mind is essential in creating a team dynamic in long form im-prov. Improv teams using Group mind allows a team to anticipate one another's moves, even finish another's sentence giving the appear-ance of having a psychic connection though the improvisers are prob-ably using empathic abilities, understanding and sharing the feelings of others or utilizing their improv training in detailed observation.

TIM WALSH BOARD GAME ENTREPRENUER
Tribond and Blurt! are two successful board games dealing with thought, that Tim invented and has marketed. Tim has traveled the world playing both games on radio and on television shows, while introducing audiences across the country to them personally. Each board game uses players' patterns of thought, in much the same way advanced improvisers use patterns of thought to build worlds on

167

stage, create relationships that play out within those worlds and to introduce the concept of game into scenes.

When our discussion turned to the mysterious connection between three seemingly unrelated activities -- jazz music, pick-up basketball, and improv, my interest was piqued. So, what do jazz music, pick-up basketball, and improv have in common? The answer is that all three use the concept of Group mind or Group think. Let's take a look at Group mind in these three activities.

GROUP MIND ON THE COURTS

I used to go down to Venice Beach in southern California and watch the guys on the courts playing pick-up ball. They'd form teams with folks they'd never played with before, and then make moves that seemed planned, as though they'd known one another and played together for years. On the court, players would work in tandem with one another, anticipating their teammates' moves. As the teams played, they made group mind decisions that amazed the spectators.

Several components of the concept seemed to be at work. First, everyone knew the game and how it was played-- which was crucial before a player even stepped out on the court. One of the improv tenants of group mind is active listening, and everyone on the courts appeared to be in a heightened listening state and in tune with the energy of everyone else on the court. Remember, active listening is listening with your whole body. The players were communicating as a hive, reacting and interacting as they moved to score points. There appeared to be group mind in action on the courts.

GROUP MIND IN JAZZ

Jazz music provides even more evidence for group mind. However, I'd first like to clarify for those non jazz folks reading this that I'm not talking about easy listening elevator jazz. I'm talking about bop, hard-bop, free form and any modern small combo jazz group that plays music utilizing extended solos and counter melodies and deviating from the basic groove or melody line at some point in the performance.

Watching an accomplished jazz combo-- they seemingly work as one. They can and often do finish or answer one another's lines. When a player is playing the melody, another knows to play a counter melody. Sometimes they play in unison. One player may start a riff, pick up on a melody line or solo at the exact point as another ends their riff. It's as though they are reading instructions on how and when to make their move, yet they're not. The combo knows when to slow down, speed up, make sudden changes in key or emotion and when to lay in the pocket feeling the groove together, while someone takes a solo.

I've seen this play out in live shows and even in the studio. One afternoon I was in the control room where Ron Carter, a veteran jazz bassist who's played on over 2,221 recordings which makes him the most recorded bassist in history, was recording. Ron was laying down a bass track alone in the studio. I watched intently as Carter would feel the rhythm of the track, listen for changes and lay into the groove, adding notes when he felt they supported the theme of the piece, as opposed to working from ego and putting in notes so that his playing would stick out. Ron Carter was listening for traces of the group mind, tuning the frequency in his brain to it, feeling it, living it.

In improv, great players use the push and pull of the scene and know just when to give or take focus. A single improviser can set the tone for others, or as Ron Carter was doing in the studio, can step in and find a way to fit comfortably into the action of the scene.

During my time in the music industry a bassist from Kingston, Jamaica, who has played in sessions with Eric Clapton, Ray Charles, Jeff Beck, Bob Marley, Jimmy Cliff and Rod Stewart, invited me to an abandoned diner, where he'd assembled a large group of session players. The musicians included multiple percussionists and horn players, jamming on Soca island melodies, giving the room a tropical feel. Everyone who played worked magically with one another. There were melodies, counter melodies and solid rhythms, supporting one another. I was able to watch and feel group mind in action. This was all done with no written music just as improvisers have no written script.

GROUP MIND IN IMPROV
Like the pick-up ball game and like jazz music, improvisers use group mind. Improvisers using group mind first must already have some level of skill at their craft. Secondly, they must be astute listeners. Yes, it does help if the improvisers have played together previously so they have a feel for each other's style of play, but that's not necessary to witness group mind in action. It just makes it easier for some improvisers to participate.

Group mind is seen and used more in long form improv where it's essential in sussing out themes, defining story lines and in pinpointing and putting games in play. In improv we know Group mind is in play when a group of improvisers allows themselves the freedom of discovery as one voice, the team as a group, looks for clues from the team members, as their scenes unfold. They use gut feeling to know when the rhythm is about to change. They sense when a member is tired or out of ideas and needs to be replaced or given a rest with another team member ready to step in.

Group mind also involves getting the clues that teammates leave during the course of a scene and putting those clues to work. You can apply the principals of Group mind to your everyday life and you'll have a clearer picture of events and others you interact with throughout your day.

Group mind is an amalgam of energies working in tandem. When a team works together, they get to know how one another think such as exploring one another's thought patterns. You've heard of an executive team that work well together in the corporate world? They're using the same principles.

So, is Group mind an energy that we can tap into? Yes. Feel your scene partner. Feel your team members. Commit to the scene and you can start to anticipate their state of play. Think, what is your scene partner trying to convey to you? Open your mind. Group mind is an unwritten bond that happens in the workplace, in family situations and with close friends. Group mind is instinct in nature.

To outside observers, group mind may appear to be a magical connection. However, group mind can be learned, and the group members must be aware and open to receiving signals from the other group members. Group mind also can lay dormant, but the well-trained improv mind can call upon it on stage as needed. Next time you watch improv, look for instances of group mind in action.

About Tim Walsh; Tim is an author and documentary filmmaker, as well as an inventor of several successful board games and full disclosure, he's my cousin. I hadn't seen Tim in years, so we had lots of catching up to do. Before inventing board games, Tim had been an athlete playing semi-pro baseball. Tim is also quite tall, and with several brothers, has had lots of experience on the courts playing pick-up basketball.

Group Mind also occurs in nature. Think of the dog pack or a flock of birds or… Well, one afternoon on the way to pick up my car…

VERVET MONKEYS ON THE MOVE
It was a beautiful afternoon at Fort Lauderdale International airport. My flight came in and I boarded a Park n' Fly shuttle for offsite long-term parking. As my shuttle rounded the corner into the long-term parking lot, the shuttle driver commented casually, that the monkeys were out. I thought, monkeys? What monkeys?!

From the shuttle window I could see several African monkeys, the type you'd see in the zoo-- Vervet Monkeys. These wild African monkeys were not in the zoo but amongst the rows of parked cars.

My wife and I got out of the shuttle and loaded suitcases into our car. There was no one else around. Thinking they were cute and might be hungry, once in my car, I pulled a bag of nuts from my backpack, wound down the window and held up a couple as an offering for the few monkeys in view. What happened next was sudden and like in a horror film-- jolting. Almost instantaneously, about 30-40 monkeys appeared from the trees that formed a forest beyond the lot. One minute there were two or three, and the next minute they were everywhere in the parking lot- in trees and on cars.

The monkeys stopped for an instant. I noticed a few glancing at one another. The monkeys appeared to be sending signals, communicating a strategy, and suddenly all were on the same page. I know this because the entire troop charged. Excited hungry monkeys can move! The monkeys were closing in and fast, as though we were in a scene from *Night of the Living Dead*.

I was in shock. It was all so surreal. The closest one suddenly was baring his teeth. Oh shit! Evidently all were hungry, and being of one mind, all were headed for me. I was the idiot waving around a small bag of nuts. What appeared initially to be a few cute creatures, now moved as one body with one thought, and the thought was to feed!

My wife screamed for me to put the window up, yelling go-go-go! I put the pedal to the metal and took off for the main road. Damn! The monkeys were practicing the art of group mind as they moved in. All on one accord, acting and thinking as one mind.

MEMORY RECALL

There's a wealth of treasures available for your scenes, locked in your mind. Reach into your nifty box! Dig deep! How do you feel about what your scene partner said? What emotions do the words or body language of your scene partner carry? Listen and react; the scene is at hand.

MY NIFTY BOX

When my mom reminisces about the past, she'll often remind me of a special box I kept as a child. It was an old cigar box that held the representative place markers associated with special memories I had growing up. I called this box my Nifty Box. At times it held an arrow-head, a piece of obsidian and a crystal. Each was worth its weight in gold to me. There were stamps, toy cars, badges, old coins and other special treasures that lived in my Nifty Box.

I'd slide my Nifty Box out from under the bed and secretly open it to explore the contents, when no one was looking. Sometimes I'd reach in and touch the treasures of my universe, feeling the energy of each item as though they were clues to that which was about to unfold in my life, as I tucked my Nifty Box under my arm and packed it back away.

Your brain is your Nifty Box. It houses the memories and treasures you hold dear. It is your box of truth. Reach into your Nifty Box, draw from it and use the senses, smells and feelings of your past to help you create in the present. Often, we refer to only a small sampling from our Nifty Box rather than the full spectrum of experiences, when we hit the improv stage.

Why do we not use the full spectrum of experiences at our fingertips? Sometimes we just tend to use go-to emotions and experiences be-cause they're easy to call on. Sometimes we are not playing as kids but as grown-ups-- blocking and protecting feelings and experiences because social norms say that grown-ups should operate on the sur-face, without revealing truths of life in the way a child would. This does no service to our improv self nor the scene we serve. Sometimes we need to take the time to unlock our thoughts and give ourselves permission to use those thoughts in our improv, to know it's okay for all of who we are to come out and play!

MEMORIES

On stage the memories in your Nifty Box, those memories that you hold dear, are the key to emotional freedom as triggers that you can call upon for your scene work.   After all improvisers are actors without a script. You have sense memory at your fingertips. You are the trapeze act without a net. Looks pretty daring! Know that when you fall-- and you will fall-- you'll be fine. Pick yourself back up. You're an improviser.

Improvisers and actors are on the same page with regard to emotion and using emotion, and the emotion connected to past experiences in scenes. Heck, while on the subject, you are not just on the same page as actors, you are an actor-- just without a script. Connect emotionally with your scene partner and with the scene itself.

Regarding connecting emotion and past experiences to scenes, acting coaches Konstantin Stanislavski, Lee Strasberg and Sanford Meisner bare this concept out in their core beliefs and methodologies.

Improv, though it relies heavily on relationships, is often hampered when improvisers step away before establishing strong emotional bonds that could take their scenes to the next level. That doesn't mean every scene should be heavy with emotion, but it does mean that great scenes showcase truthful feelings and emotions. We sometimes rob ourselves of great scene work by not being more available for the scene.

Stanislavski believed actors need to take emotion and personality to the stage, and to store it and make it available for characters to call upon when needed during a scene. Stanislavski was the first in the West to see acting as more than physical and vocal training. His goal was to find ways to activate an actor's subconscious behavior.

Lee Strasberg made emotional recall the basis for "method acting". His methodology has been utilized by many great actors such as Marlon Brando.

Sanford Meisner-- with his Meisner approach to acting-- calls on actors to "get out of their head" and be present and available to behave instinctively. Isn't this what improv is about? Don't the following improv terms apply: Be in the moment. Commit! Be truthful. Be passionate! Get out of your head!

Reach into your Nifty Box. Ask yourself what discoveries there are that might enhance the scene. Opening yourself up to playing as a child is a great start. Allow yourself to freely experience in the moment emotions. Next, feel free to reach in and explore the emotions and events of the past. Improvisers are only bound by the limitations we put on ourselves. Use your Nifty Box.

CHALLENGE

This exercise is for a group of improvisers. Make a back line. Ask for a suggestion of an idiom, a proverb or an adage. To clarify: a proverb often has a piece of advice, while an adage merely states a general truth, and an idiomatic expression is made up of words that have a meaning not deducible from those of the individual words themselves-- such as "It Takes Two to Tango."

From the suggestion, each improviser in the back line comes up with a related saying that is personal to them. For example, if the suggestion was "It Takes Two to Tango," one improviser might choose "I shouldn't have skipped school." Another might say "You encouraged me to take the key." The saying is personal to you. Remember, your line should be based on your life and past experiences or beliefs.

The entire backline takes a few steps forward with each improviser chanting his or her personal saying at the same time, over and over. This will sound like cacophony to some. After about six to eight chants, everyone steps back but two improvisers. The two take turns going back and forth, taking turns repeating their personalized sayings, three to five more times, before starting a scene together.

By beginning the scene with one of the sayings, your scene will be personalized. This will also help with giving both scene partners a solid point of view. Once the two on stage have had a short scene, they step back, and the group as a whole moves forward, with everyone saying their own line at the same time as before, leaving two more improvisers to do a scene together.

ROLE PLAYING

The night I met Prince I was role playing. We often role play in improv. My persona that evening--my character so to speak-- was rooted in truth, and embraced by me from the outside in. I was on a mission, and unbeknownst to me when the evening began, I would allow what I wore and how I carried myself to affect my place in the scene, as that scene unfolded around me, and I found myself face to face with The Purple One.

In improv, we are always role playing. Some improv schools teach big character choices that involve changing up all the aspects of physicality in order to get the character you've created across to the audience. That school of thought teaches you to change your walk, your speech patterns, the tonal quality of your speech, your character's posture, facial expressions and reaction time to outside stimuli, etc.

Another school of thought regarding characters in improv takes the focus away from physicality and speech patterns and adheres to a more muted approach. When an improviser merely shows themselves doing an activity-- they are that character. For example, I might stand over an imaginary operating table and ask a nurse for a scalpel. Therefore, I am a surgeon. As an improviser, I am playing the role of a surgeon with the truth that only I myself (Greg), can bring my essence to the character I am playing. The layers of personality of my character might come out in the scene, but I wouldn't necessarily create a character with over the top traits.

Neither school of thought is right. Neither is wrong. Whatever style fits the scene you are discovering and supports your scene partner, is the right choice. In either case, you are role playing. Improv is about role playing. Keep in mind that what serves the scene serves you! We will get into the specifics of character creation in another post. Here we will look at the role and the energy that puts us in the role.

THE ROLLS AND THE ROLE

In my 20s, my day job was as an administrative assistant in network prime-time programming. I'd occasionally take outside jobs to supplement my income. One weekend, a high-rolling, specialty car importer to the stars, hired me to chauffeur partygoers in his Vintage Rolls Royce Silver Cloud. My mission-- should I accept it-- was to drive Hollywood cognoscenti--those climbing the industry ladder and a few on the outside licking the glass-- to a party in northern Malibu.

The afternoon of the party, I picked up the car in town, only to discover the brakes were soft and I was about to pick up guests in the hills for an hour drive out to the party. I also discovered that the owner had no insurance and mine would not have covered a Rolls. I slid behind the steering wheel that evening, decked in a conservative dark navy pinstripe wool suit-- courtesy of Brooks Bros and a yard sale in the upscale Holmby Hills neighborhood south of Bel Air and north of UCLA.

The suit added a few years to my young, slender frame. I could pass as a young studio exec. After hustling several carloads of mostly single women ready for their screen debut, and several agents and managers to the party, I settled in at the party, waiting by the front door on a padded bench. I felt out of place in my conservative heavy wool suit but was ready to spring into action if my driving prowess was needed.

THE AGENT

I'd been sitting for quite some time when an agent asked for a lift back into town. About 30-40 minutes into our drive, my passenger requested we stop at a night club in mid-city L.A. I was unsure whether we should take the detour, but he assured me our host would never notice my being gone a few minutes extra. I'd been told to serve the guests' needs, and so I did. Feeling overdressed in my conservative pin-striped suit when we arrived at the club, I offered to wait by the car. The agent persisted that I should accompany him inside, and I relented. He also promised to pay my cover and introduce me around the club, which he did. I'm still not sure why, although I suspect he was hoping I'd role play, which I did.

TO ROLE PLAY WITH PRINCE
There was a long line outside the club, but the door man walked us to the front of the line and let us in with no cover. It was at that point I realized I could utilize my good fortune of having dressed as an executive. I was in a role and about to improvise.

We made our way to the back of the crowded club, where the artist known as Prince was waiting. Prince was dressed in a very purple suit with no shirt that included a suit jacket designed like tux tails with straight leg trousers tapered to a tighter fit around his ankles. The Purple One had just completed the film *Purple Rain*, and though it was not yet released, the film was expected to do well at the box office. We shook hands and attempted to converse, but the music was loud. I smiled and mouthed some words. Prince was very polite.

I also met a couple members of his band as well. I could only hear every other word over the pounding club music as I mouthed compliments and attempted bits of conversation. Prince stayed attentive. He seemed to assume I was a studio exec, and I did nothing to dissuade him. I was in the moment and standing tall in an executive like stance. The whole situation was surreal and could have been a scene from an improv class.

After shaking hands, Prince seemed to look for my card and I feigned that I was all out. When we were finished at the club, I took the agent home, making that same long, hour plus journey back to the party in Malibu, where I planted myself back in that same seat by the front door, well into the wee hours of the morning racking up a big pay day. I left the party and my new young executive persona at about 4:30 A.M. It had been a long night. I went home feeling authentically tired, and after driving the Rolls without proper insurance, felt true stress just as a studio executive might feel-- though for other reasons. Now that's role playing!

As an improviser, when you take on a role, there are times when the scene dictates its needs and creates the character. There are also times when you play a role and the scene unfolds around that role. As an improviser you are always in a role on stage. Play the role truthfully and you'll have the audience in your hand.

WHEN IN DOUBT-- IMPROVISE
My role in the real world that evening was driver, chauffeur, or maybe even guest relations. My role in the world of the scene as I approached Prince, was that of a young executive paying homage to a new voice, an up and coming star. I was a character that evening, which had been built from the "outside in", using the traits of executives I'd seen in action while on my day job as an administrative assistant in the network television executive suites of Century City. Donning a conservative winter weight wool suit, I set my character in motion-- that is, when I put on the outfit, I stepped into the character from the "outside in".

CHARACTERS FROM THE OUTSIDE IN or THE INSIDE OUT?
Do you build your characters from the "inside" out or from the "outside" in? Have you done both? Improvisers for the most part build characters from the inside out. Let's look at a couple of examples. Johnny Depp is an outside in actor. When Johnny puts on the costume, it pushes him into character. He's influenced by his surroundings which he then funnels into the characters he's developing. On the other hand, Marlon Brando was an inside out actor. Brando internalized his characters with or without a costume, releasing them during the scene. Brando's costumes and surroundings really didn't influence his character.

Is "outside in" character development or "inside out" character development better? The answer is that neither is better than the other. Each are just a means to an end. Two different methodologies of developing characters.

CHALLENGE

Take a moment here. Ask yourself. Do your characters come alive when you put on a period costume, character appropriate clothing and/or make-up to fit a specific role, or do you need no costume at all to feel a role? Before you answer, rewind the past few characters you've played, and look at the details that lay before you.

I was playing a role rooted in truth the evening I met Prince, and doing so with commitment, and that's why it worked. I was also working from the outside in. Take a look at some of your favorite actors. Are they "outside in" actors or "inside out" actors? Make a list. Which ones do you relate to? What are you? Perhaps a little of both. Hopefully as an improviser you work well "inside out" since improvisers aren't in costumes often.

CARVE YOUR STEP

Make your mark! When you make your mark on stage by carving a step, you are leaving a foothold for your improv scene partner or your teammates waiting in the wings. You not only show your creative genius, you provide the footing for others to step into and raise themselves a little higher. Carving a step for others illustrates the improv adage: when you make your scene partner look good, you look good!

You may carve your step in real life also. However, when you've given all you can and it appears you may not make it through the night, carving that last step carries a bit more weight. Let me illustrate.

JAMAICAN TERROR
His right side was numb, but he managed to drag himself to a back bedroom. Reggae drummer Carlton Santa Davis had been shot. He nearly bled out, as his life flashed before his eyes, while waiting for an ambulance to arrive.

With credits that read like a history of Jamaican music, Carlton Davis was the go-to drummer on the reggae scene for years, performing or recording with Bob Marley & the Wailers, Sly & Robbie, The Mighty Diamonds, the Aggrovators, Sugar Minot, Roots Radics, Soul Syndicate and Big Youth. Davis also performed on solo records for original Wailers Peter Tosh and Denise Brown, as well as the godfather of reggae King Tubby. Carlton Davis was and still is the back beat of traditional reggae music.

The night he was shot, Davis had been visiting Peter Tosh, a founding member of the Wailers, Bob Marley's band. Gangsters forced their way into Tosh's Jamaican home. There were three men-- one wielding an M16 rifle and two others with handguns who ordered Tosh's dinner guests to "belly up" (lay face down on the floor). Without provocation the three-armed men began executing the guests, one at a time. Three died with shots to the head including Tosh. Davis was shot in the upper torso and barely survived.

Doctors were unsure of when or even if Davis would ever play again. He no longer had the use of his right side and was told the healing process would be a painful, arduous process. I met Carlton Santa Davis eight years later in Los Angeles, where he'd traveled to get away from the dark memories of that night.

I'd been hired to produce an alternative rock act, straight forward and easy enough, but then was told the act would include a rhythm section made up of reggae artists from Jamaica. It was a unique approach. How would the styles meld?

While I found recording a Jamaican rhythm section in a way that that would meld with an aggressive alternative rock sound to be a challenge, Davis made the musical journey at hand, a pleasant one. Even with all his experience and impressive credits, Davis checked his ego at the door, focusing on the task at hand. Carlton Davis was so at home in the studio that he relaxed others. Here was a man still healing from a traumatic injury-- as much mental as physical-- working in a musical environment a bit outside his normal sphere. Yet Davis still made his mark by providing support and encouragement to others on the session.

As an improviser, be the steady support player. Carve your step and provide the piece that others can build on. You will not only have better scenes, but you'll be the improviser everyone will want to share the stage with. With each step you take on stage, with each move, create a path for those behind you to follow.

The alt rock/reggae project turned out to be a bit too outside the norm for the public and fell into the musical abyss where obscure projects go for the big sleep. However, for a moment, a man had provided a leg up for others. The world needs more of that. Carlton Davis carved his step and lit the way.

CAMP STORIES

As a child I'd gone away to camp. One camp story that stuck with me over the years is about a group of boys and their guide, hiking in the mountains. They make camp, and one of the boys ends up wandering off during a snowstorm, eventually falling into a pit with seemingly no way out. There are skeletons littering the floor of the pit and on the wall of the pit are stick figures counting sunrises and sunsets.

The boy discovers the beginning of toe hold carvings in the walls of the pit where he can get a foothold. He starts toward the top. The bottom carvings are well defined. They're cut far into the wall of the pit. As the boy climbs higher, he finds that the carvings are not only less deep, but they only reach little more than halfway up the side of the pit.

The boy will have to start carving where someone else left off in order for him to reach the top. Next to the final carved out toe hold, someone has taken a rock or knife and etched in the wall of the pit "carve your step". That's where the boy must begin his carvings.

Working for days, he continues the carvings working his way toward the top of the pit. After several days in the pit he's so tired and weak from hunger he makes what he thinks will be his last carving. At this point he's figuring he won't make it out. However, the boy hasn't paid attention to how many steps he's carved, nor how high up the pit he's been working. He's been merely building upon what was there. Using his last bit of energy, the boy makes it to the top and is able to pull himself out. He realizes he made it out because he built on what others had started.

If your scene partner gives you a gift, be it a tool, or any concept you can build on, use that gift and add to it, build on it. Make your mark. Carve your step.

MAGIC IN IMPROV

POWERS OF CREATION

I remember reading that Beatle John Lennon had said that he understands the craft of songwriting and can sit down and write a song as a technical exercise. But when Lennon sits at the piano or with a guitar and allows a song to flow through him and to write itself, the final product is so much greater. That is exactly how great improv flows. Couldn't you say the process for creation itself is magical?!

Improv is magical. Think about it. You as an improviser, have the magical powers of creation at your fingertips. Improvisers bring characters of all types to life, and then give them their personalities as well as decide how they should dress, where they live and what their social status is.

Improvisers don't just create characters either, improvisers create towns, cities and worlds! Take a moment to marinate in the magic of your creative power as an improviser. It's awe-inspiring and it's unlimited.

Improvisers can also use this magical energy of creation to endow the characters they've brought to life on stage and even those of their scene partner. An improviser might be in a scene and decide to endow their scene partner with a limp, a sexy smile or a specific attitude. Take a moment to realize you have these abilities, claim your magic and empower yourself!

Aside from the creation of buildings and people and endowing characters, and improvisers have the seven magical realms of improv at their fingertips. Each of the seven realms defy the laws of our everyday life and yet exist as a truth in the world of the stage.

THE SEVEN MAGICAL REALMS OF IMPROV

There are seven distinct magical realms in improv. The concepts these seven realms embrace often directly affect the comedic or dramatic outcome in scenes. You have probably already used a few of these concepts if not all seven though you may never have looked closely at them. The seven realms are;

(1) **Talking with the dead:** In improv we often chat with the departed in scenes. You've probably never given this subject much thought, but on an improv stage you can sing, dance and romance the dead, all in the same scene-- and it's acceptable. You can have an emotional poignant scene or a hilarious one born out of what some see as a silly concept. It can also be a poignant one. The creative outcome achieved by talking with the dead is endless. I get my best recipes from the departed, at least one of my characters does.

(2) **The use of power objects:** Power objects can affect the characters created by improv scene partners, thus affecting the general direction of the scene, in either a positive or negative manner. Using a power object involves focusing energy on the power object and that energy has a causal effect on the scene's outcome. Power objects have been used in films for years. Some of the screens greatest actors are quite skilled at identifying and using them. The same principal can be applied to objects on the improv stage to achieve a comedic or dramatic outcome.

(3) **Travel through time and space:** In improv all things are possible. There are unlimited dimensions in which to travel. Therefore, I say travel across time and through space more often! There is much to see, do and experience. Think of the many creative uses of time travel in improv. The key is to play the experience seriously while using the addition of this concept opens up worlds of comedic possibilities!

(4) **Group mind:** Group mind or group think, puts the entire team on the same page, operating as one mind. It's also magical. You, for example, might finish your scene partner's sentence. Are you showcasing psychic ability or just familiarity with your team member's state of play? You want the audience to experience the team working together and on one accord. Is that magic or skill? There

are greater possibilities for success in your scene work through Group mind and a satisfaction that goes with knowing all pistons are firing at the same time. Bring on the magic of Group mind!

(5) **Giving innate objects and/or animals human attributes:** Isn't this already taking place in nature at least with animals? Animals are getting smarter. It's a scientific fact. Animals are showing their emotions as well and scientists are discovering that many species once thought to possess little intelligence are smarter than originally thought. In improv, innate objects and/or animals have needs and wants and can discuss them in conversation. It doesn't get much more magical than that! We've already established that many animals have high intelligence. Build on that fact for brilliant scenes.

(6) **Accepting the unusual and/or impossible as truth:** In the world of the scene improvisers often accept the unusual or impossible as truth. Justification of those concepts in the world of the scene changes the laws of physics giving us an otherworldly outlook on life. In my classes, I hammer the concept of two worlds. They are the world of the scene and the world of our everyday lives. Some truths exist in both worlds and others only exist in the world of the scene because they defy the science of our everyday lives. Yet, the scene has embraced those unusual concepts as truths by justifying their use in the world of the scene. Walla! Magic!

(7) **Creating worlds:** Improvisers create worlds, filling them with all the tools needed to envision great scene work. Creating these worlds is done with the wave of a hand, flick of a wrist or by speaking a few words as though we are creators of the realm. An improviser can walk on stage and transform that space into a world where plants eat people and people communicate telepathically or communicate in sign language and it all happens in a world of extreme heat or cold. Once again, the magic of Improv at work!

Each of the magical concepts above would be considered quite normal if they appeared in an improv scene. On the other hand, their appearance in your everyday life, would probably create quite a stir. Think about how you might use the above tools effectively in a scene. Take your time and digest the information. Now create a world in your mind and give it life. You can travel to that world without blinking an eye using thought. Improv truly is magical.

THOUGHTS ARE THINGS

Thoughts are things. Of course, we can't see them, but we can feel their essence as spoken words and feel the energy they carry whether positive or negative. We rarely if ever, ask ourselves, where did the initial thought come from before it manifested in the physical? Perhaps the thought was an impulse reaction to a scene partner's actions or an emotional reaction to a "gift" from a scene partner that demanded an emotional response. It could even be a connection to the past triggered by something that happened in the scene. In improv, thinking of thoughts as things will strengthen your scene work.

Characters in an improv scene take action to achieve a goal or goals based on their belief system, their status or their hunger for attention. They have wants and emotional connections to other characters. These thoughts like the thought of a character want, come from our creative unconscious. It's a muscle-improvisers use often.

In secret societies, magicians (aka the Magi or Magus), share a connection to and manipulation of thought. Therefore, they must have been early improvisers, right?! Thought is energy. Thought manifests into action which manifests into the physical. However, improvisers can just make stuff appear in their world of the stage. As an improviser, when you do really explore what you've created, live in it and let it affect the scene.

Improvisers can have fun with magical aspects of the scene, by taking serious subject matter and giving it a twist, or seeing an event, place or person differently by having an unusual viewpoint. In a scene, let's say your mother has just passed and she comes to you at night. You sit up in bed and without fear might say, "Ma, I was hoping you'd come. I lost your chicken soup recipe."

OBJECTS CARRY ESSENCE
Every object you create for use in an improv scene has an essence. Just as an object does in the world of your everyday life. Objects in the world of your everyday life as well as in the world of the stage, have dimensions, texture, size, weight and other unique characteristics that define the object. Through object work improvisers create and re-create objects giving these items their essence and in turn using them in the scene. For example, in an improv scene that has one character wearing a watch to work, we first create that watch in our mind using our imagination, and then manifest the watch in the scene using object work. The scene feels the essence of the object, and that essence in turn, is felt by others in the scene as the characters in the scene use the object one of them just created.

In long form improv, performing an action in one scene creates a texture in the scene that often resonates later in that same scene, or may even resonate in another separate scene, because that action leaves energy residue in the scene. In improv long form terms, what you set up on the first beat, will be felt in a later beat.

POWER OBJECTS

Power objects come in all sizes and shapes. You'll find them in the most obvious places-- on your dresser, by your nightstand, in your jewelry box, or even in the all -purpose kitchen junk drawer. The power object could even be your jewelry box. Power objects can literally be just about anything. More than the object itself though, it's the improviser who labels the power object, which happens as they use it as a power object.

Imagine that it's Friday night and you've finished work and are at home putting on your favorite pair of jeans or rummaging through your closet for that special pair of shoes to wear for a night out. The following Monday, you're putting on your 'lucky' tie for a business presentation, or maybe you've taken the day off and are taking your favorite guitar out of its case for a practice session.

Any of the items in the situations I've begun to describe can be power objects. Power objects are power objects because the improviser or actor has chosen that item to focus energy on which will have an effect on the outcome of the scene.

In an improv scene, the power objects are a focus point or energy hot spot in the scene. Picture a guy who is making an attempt at being romantic with his girlfriend when the pizza delivery company keeps calling and interrupting, and the guy becomes more focused on receiving a free pizza if the delivery is late, than on the woman he's on a date with. His phone is the power object. Then there's the important business meeting where one of the principals in a suit, seated at the decision makers table, is so focused on getting the right amount of sweetener in his coffee that it becomes noticeable. The sweetener is the power object. Maybe getting the right amount of sweetener is not the focus point in the scene, but his coffee is so good he just sighs with delight intermittently, during the CEO's strategy talk. In this instance his coffee is the power object.

WEAPONS OF POWER

When the power object is used, it can be an innocent diversion, such as the guy who keeps straightening a picture instead of paying attention to others in the scene or a weapon of power. One example might be the cell phone that keeps going off and interrupting the scene's two improvisers, who are having normal interaction. The power object as a weapon of power can also be something that's utilized in the scene, for example the printer that only prints wrong documents. The weapon of power might also be a purse that carries every tool known to man except what is needed to solve the issue-- which happens several times during the scene.

When I played the punk clubs in NYC including Max's Kansas City, CBGB's and Club 57 at Irving Plaza, my band often opened for major acts. Any one of many objects with me related to the show was a possible power object. As a scene partner, I could easily put my energy into music, my guitar, the clothes I wore on stage, the individual band members interacting on stage or our raucous show. They were all important elements. More often than not, my actual power object(s) were one of two 1950s department store mannequins I set up on stage. All power objects are objects the improviser focuses energy on though it could be in different unique ways.

My Marshall 100-watt half stack (guitar amp) had a headless torso lashed to the Marshall's amp head like a victim tied to the railroad tracks by a villain. In front of my rig stood a male mannequin dressed as a person. These two objects were a defining focal point for the band's quirky energy, and a motivation for our fans to join the fray on the dance floor. Were they the reason Chrysalis records sent an executive to check out our show and consider signing us? No. If I were to keep coming back to them as a focal point in some way then they could be.

POWER OBJECTS IN TV

My first introduction to power objects was in a Hollywood scene study acting class, where actors watched several pieces of film and then were instructed to focus on the lead actors to see if they were focusing energy on objects in the scene. Then, we were to more closely examine what power objects, if any, they might be using, and how the power object in the scene was affecting the scene. What I observed is that when an actor in a film uses a power object, it is done so below the surface.

Television commercials can be a great inspirational tool for viewing power objects in use. In the world of advertising, the first rule is that commercials sell feelings not items, and brands use feelings to get people to buy. How many commercials have you seen in which a product creates a feeling? When you think about it though, probably a lot…

When an improviser chooses to add a power object to a scene, they can use the object to create an emotional connection, in much the same way commercials do by repeating use of the item throughout the scene. Remember a power object's energy actually comes from the improviser's character's energy, not the object itself.

The power object is merely a focus for the improviser's power. Think about a guy on a date, and every time his date begins talking seriously about their relationship, he takes out his cell phone to inquire when the pizza he ordered is going to arrive. The more he uses his phone, the greater urgency in his voice, and the more the scene is heightened.

CHALLENGE
Try a series of two person scenes where one of two improvisers utilize an object in the scene as a power object. The improviser that introduces the object should not say anything about the actual object. Each time the object comes into focus, explore heightening the action of the scene after something happens. For example, a guy on break is playing cards for money. Every time he looks at the clock to check when his break is up, he loses another $20. After the scene, ask your scene partner if they can name what the power object is or was, and discuss how it affected the scene and why. Power objects are a focal

point that allow the improviser's energy to come out. The object only is a power object because the improviser is focused in some way on the chosen object.

Think duck-duck-goose game theory by introducing the power object, then going back to the everyday reality of the scene. Then let the object affect the scene, then go back to the everyday reality of the scene again. When the improviser brings the power object back into the scene a second or third time, let its introduction each time affect the scene at an even greater amount than the previous time. Explore this concept. There are many ways power objects can be used. Explore.

PLAYING ANIMALS

Playing animals that are living the human experience on earth, yet exhibiting animal traits, is an interesting study of both animal and human behavior and can lead to a very funny scene. The trick is to let your inner beast bubble to the surface. Often improvisers try to complicate the process when the key is to simply be yourself but with the traits of an Otter, Cow, Lion, House Cat or whatever creature you're portraying on stage.

THERE'S A CRANE ON MY CAR
The other day I left breakfast to be greeted by a lone crane standing in the center of my car's roof. As the breeze rustled through his feathers, the crane turned to me lifting one leg while focusing his eyes on me. I'd seen him earlier on a table just outside the restaurant I'd been dining in. Staring at the customers, with his beak pressed up against the front window his eyes called out, "feed me, I gotta eat too." I could see familiar traits of a distant relative in my feathered friend's actions.

One afternoon I looked up from my South Florida back porch at the power lines to see a squirrel and a large bright green Cuban Aloe lizard facing off. The squirrel eventually gave in after locating an alternate route on an adjacent power line. The scene played out like two schoolboys fighting for playground dominance over some unimportant issue that seemed vital at the time. It brought my mind back to elementary school and playground antics that went unseen by the teaching staff.

DUCKS & MORE DUCKS
Recently a pair of large Muscovy ducks greeted me in front of my house. Originating from South America, Muscovy ducks have been in the states 100 years, so they should qualify as naturalized citizens. The government, however, still considers them invasive immigrants. In Florida, since they began as pets released in the wild, they don't even get wildlife protections afforded other wildlife. *"Oh my god! A duck family just moved into my neighborhood!"* They are the poster children for turbulent social interaction on the streets of any city USA,

illustrating how our waterfowl are at times treated with disrespect just because they're waterfowl.

I first encountered the same pair of Muscovy Ducks several days ago, as they were playing in a puddle after a brief rain. I walked to a nearby palm that had a cluster of low hanging ripe palm berries. Ducks enjoy the palm berries ripe husks. Having keen memories and recalling my kindness from a previous encounter I had with them, they quickly waddled over to me there on the lawn. The larger duck stopped within an arm's length of me, and began wagging his tail, in much the same manner as a happy canine greets his master. Unable to return the greeting effectively, I led them back over to the palm berries, shaking down several riper berries for them to snack on. They ate the red husks.

LIZARDS

Last year, a three-legged Curly Tail lizard would track my movements whenever I came out the back door. During the summer months, I would turn on the hose and spray him. The lizard would dip its head and wash its face, enjoying the cool water. Some days, my three-legged friend would stand on a sprinkler head in front of me, or on a plant near my leg, making sure I'd seen him. This action reminded me of the days when Dad would come home from a day at work, and my sister and I would vie for his attention.

Animals are social creatures just like we are, and just like humans, animals have unique personalities and varying degrees of awareness. That being said, animals are much smarter than we humans give them credit for being. Some animals may be as smart as, if not smarter than, humans. Now if I had to name one thing my animal encounters and/or observations have had in common, it's that animals are a gold mine for improv ideas. They're a gold mine for improv ideas because in them I see bits of myself and my friends, family and co-workers.

PLAYING ANIMALS AS ANIMALS

There are two clear paths for playing animals in improv. Improvisers have the option of safely playing animals as we might observe them in the wild such as cows in a pasture or sheep baying in a field. When playing animals in this manner, as humans view them in the wild, the improviser is usually playing the animal this way to create a stage picture. The animal in this kind of scene is a background actor. Therefore, it's appropriate to make animal noises and crawl around the stage as long as your animal character doesn't take away from the characters in the scene that are speaking.

This type of animal portrayal is helpful when there is one or several improvisers in a long form scene, and there is a reference to a pet or farm animal. Playing an animal as humans view them in the wild is most effective as a background tool. It's sometimes not that exciting, but the animal is being used as a set piece or something to work off of or react to.

PLAYING ANIMALS LIVING THE HUMAN EXPERIENCE

The other way of playing animals on stage takes a bit more imagination. It's basically what we see in animated animal films these days. The animals appear to have a combination of both human and animal characteristics. The animals speak like humans-- love, complain, and anger just as humans, but they show animal traits.

Imagine how much more interesting it is for you as an improviser and your audience, if you play animals that speak as humans and have human characteristics melded with animal traits. The audience can then become voyeurs into the animal's personal lives. You could have a couple of dogs complaining about the lack of females in the neighborhood or the lack of freedom on their walk. They could even have human hobbies like stamp collecting. The possibilities are limitless.

Observing animals interacting with other animals gives us clues as to how they might behave and how they might sound if they could talk. How we play animals is limited only by the limits on our imagination.

Observing animals interacting with humans is even more engaging. Squirrels for example, can be quite interesting.

THE HUNGRY CA COFFEE SPOT SQUIRREL

A favorite coffee spot of mine in Los Angeles, located near the studios, is home to a one-eyed squirrel. At certain times of day, the back patio of an unnamed cafe becomes the courtyard of fear. Perhaps the deranged rodent is a frustrated actor angling for a screen test.

This one eyed rodent, also missing a paw, scurries along the top of a tall wooden fence around the courtyard of the outdoor cafe seeking his next meal. This marauding terror drops down on unsuspecting diners to snatch scraps from their plates. Sometimes he even bares his teeth, taking a swipe at customers with his stub, to get access to a snack. Whether just frustrated and hungry, or a tortured furry soul haunting patrons and in search of reprisal, the patio is his domain.

One morning I'd just gotten my order and was looking for a seat when I spotted the squirrel out of the corner of my eye. He seemed to be on the hunt. I thought, how cute. The person I'd come to meet warned me against sitting too close to the wooden fence surrounding the courtyard. I paid the warning no mind.

As I sat down, I looked up to see the one-eyed squirrel scampering down from the top of the fence with demonic focus in his one good eye. He was coming for me. As he took the stance to leap down on my plate, I snatched it, and stood up, turning my plate from him. I moved to a table toward the middle of the courtyard. As I stood up, he bared his teeth. I'd barely saved my meal from him.

Animals are smart and they seem to be getting smarter. Over the years, I've seen them take on more and more human traits, or perhaps we are taking on their traits. The challenge for improvisers playing animals is to play them with enough human traits that the audience has a clear picture of animals having human emotional interaction, and yet clearly seeing that the improviser is playing an animal.

On stage, we can give the animals personalities with wants and goals that drive their behavior-- from hunger, to age, to upper or lower class. We can portray animals as slobs, or as having OCD, or being addicted, as being studious and/or having fervent political viewpoints. What better way to explore social norms than through animals!

IQ CREDIT WHERE CREDIT IS DUE
In the animal kingdom here on earth, crows for example, can count, differentiate between complex shapes, and do observational learning tasks. They've been observed making a knife for slicing food. When several are present, if they're living a life of crime, you'll see one is busy thieving, another acts as lookout, while a third acts as a decoy. Rats are also highly intelligent and can show signs of excitement, loss, stress and remorse, while the African Grey parrot, the sixth most intelligent animal, has the intelligence of a 5-year-old child. The smartest mammal of all is the Orangutan. They can observe humans using a saw to build something, and then they will use the saw be-cause they not only understand the task they're learning, but also why humans use that skill and when it is appropriate to do so.

There are times when playing animals as animals is the right choice. Sometimes a shepherd in a scene needs a sheep that doesn't talk and just does sheep-like things. When we play animals as animals that don't speak or have human characteristics, it's usually to support a human character. Be careful not to upstage the human if you are doing so. Just remember how interesting it is to see two crows in a card game. *"Remember if I win this hand, I take the pot and the loser gets time out on the Scarecrow!"*

CHALLENGE
Watch some nature programs on television. Observe the behavior and stereotypical traits unique to a certain breed of animal. What traits would define their archetype? Next make a list of human social situations and general behavior that might happen in those situations. Now combine the two. How would a penguin behave at a wedding, or deer that were members of a hunting lodge? Imagine a badger and a turtle enjoying a beer together. The turtle probably nurses his beer.

He might hide in his shell when an attractive person walks by. The badger might have an aggressive personality that comes out in the scene.

Observe animals, observe nature. Make yourself aware of its rhythm. Store the details in your brain. Use them onstage. You might see animals act in a way you can use in a scene between two humans. What animals have you observed lately? Yes, I know humans are animals. Playing those other animals, the ones in the forest, is challenging and fun.

CHALLENGE
Create several animals in your mind. Give them a back story, with wants and personality. Write the info down in a notebook. Introduce your animal character to another improviser's animal character and then let the other improviser introduce their animal character to yours.

THE FINAL SCENE

DISCOVER THE SCENE

Every day I step out into the world, there is a new scene to be impro-vised and each scene is a new adventure. By using the concepts in this book, I navigate my everyday life with greater success as well as improve the quality of my improv performances on stage.

Improv can be applied to every aspect of daily life, just as you can apply every aspect of your daily life to improv. To really grow your game, become one with the scene, take the time to breathe it in. Let the scene fill your lungs...As you breathe it in, note that the scene has a flow and rhythm the same as life itself. To truly discover this scene, you must surrender to both your scene partner and to the scene itself. This is a big ask for many improvisers because it in-volves trust in your partner and that he or she will strive to make you look good.

The first half of the title of this book, "Life improvised", addresses the unwritten rules of improv. These unwritten rules apply to your work on the stage as well as the relationships and scenes that play out in your everyday life. They are the basic tenants of improv. These basic tenants of improv set the parameters from which great improv un-folds.

The other half of the title, "Listening Between the Lines", addresses the improvisers ability to listen beyond words and hear what's NOT being said verbally. By tuning into the emotions that travel with the words spoken, as well as deciphering any actions or movements that accompany those words, improvisers can listen between the lines. It's like looking at a stereogram - those 3-D pictures that hang in mod-ern art museums. The focused improviser sees the picture that exists within the picture.

Relationships are an important component of a strong improv scene. When you meet someone for the first time your gut tells you something about that person. Some of us reflect upon that information automatically. Others must make a conscious effort to do so. Either way our subconscious picks up information and then is hard at work deciphering that information whether we realize this or not.

The question remains, is the energy your subconscious is picking up a momentary blip based on how your day has been going or have you tapped into something. If you just take the time to observe your scene partners posture, movement, voice timbre and the way they carry themselves, you can know their intent. Read, analyze, detect. You may have a feeling for their true nature because you're listening between the lines.

AN IMPERFECT LIFE
We all make mistakes. We make mistakes on stage and in life. Improv helps us see our mistakes, correct them and occasionally make fun of them. Sometimes you learn from those mistakes and other times the lessons repeat themselves providing an endless cycle, until you learn whatever lesson you were meant to learn. Improv can provide you with the awareness to not repeat a lesson too often.

The more you immerse yourself in improv the more you learn about yourself. Be prepared for this learning experience. It can be disconcerting at first. Stay with the process and getting to know yourself will be exciting. Learning to love yourself is even more of an adventure. They're both part of the journey of being an improviser. You'll also discover how to tap into your funny.

Then there's the matter of creating characters for the stage. There are many approaches. Improv characters like people are multi-layered. Often a simple one-dimensional character takes on multi-dimensional facets as a scene plays out and the characters discover themselves and their scene partners, through the skewed lens of improv. The skewed lens of improv being defined as seeing and experiencing the world through unique and varied vantage points.

While on stage you may play a military commander in one scene and a car thief in another. In your everyday life you play various characters as well. You may not always realize it because you do so without thinking. You probably won't play a heart surgeon in the morning and a car mechanic in the afternoon, but you could be cast in the role of a child, a parent and an employee on the same day.

For those who find creating characters on stage challenging look at how often you change characters quickly without even giving it a second thought. I've played a father, son, teacher collector and boss all in a single day. How many characters do you play in a day?

Today, improv scenes often take on the same casual format of non-connection that we as grown adults, perpetrate in our everyday lives when dealing with other adults. We interact at a distance rather than allowing our characters to intimately connect. We gloss over life, existing only on the surface. Often our real-life scenes are polite, non-confrontational and without depth or meaning. There's nothing more boring than watching a polite, non-confrontational improv scene and it's not healthy in life either. Connect with your scene partner!

MY STORY
Every one of the stories used to illustrate an improv concept in this book could have been your story. They all involve a relationship, an attitude and two scene partners dedicated to that scene with the passion and commitment needed to experience it fully.

Some of the stories in this book involve celebrities. I happened to have worked in entertainment. My stories could just as easily have been stories about a hair stylist, computer programmer, gardener, chef or car mechanic. Perhaps yours are. However, the stories in this book are my stories and are the stories of a lifetime of relationships and the ups and downs that provided my lessons. Just as these stories showcase my happiness, sadness, success, disappointment and every feeling in between, they are the stories of a Life Improvised. What's your story? Scene...

www.ingramcontent.com/pod-product-compliance
Lightning Source LLC
Chambersburg PA
CBHW071426090426
42737CB00011B/1576